Co-dependency:
Issues in Treatment
and Recovery

ABOUT THE EDITORS

Bruce Carruth, PhD, is a social worker in private practice in Little Rock, Arkansas, where he specializes in the treatment of chemically dependent families. In addition to being editor of the *Journal of Chemical Dependency Treatment*, he is also Senior Editor for the Haworth Series in Addictions Treatment. Dr. Carruth was formerly the director of the Alcoholism Training Program at the University of Arkansas Medical School, and before moving to Arkansas, he was on the faculty of Rutgers University Center of Alcohol Studies. In addition to his clinical practice, Dr. Carruth regularly leads workshops for chemical dependency and mental health professionals throughout the United States.

Warner Mendenhall, PhD, is a professor at the University of Akron, Wayne College in Akron, Ohio. He specializes in the treatment of chemically dependent and co-dependent persons and their families in his private psychotherapy practice, also in Akron. He also conducts an extensive eight-day co-dependency treatment program. As Executive Director, Education and Counseling Service, Inc., Akron, Ohio, he trains counselors and physicians to diagnosis chemically dependent and co-dependent persons. Dr. Mendenhall spends his summers in New Jersey as a faculty member at Rutgers University Center of Alcohol Studies.

Co-dependency: Issues in Treatment and Recovery

Bruce Carruth
Warner Mendenhall
Editors

The Haworth Press
New York • London

Co-dependency: Issues in Treatment and Recovery has also been published as *Alcoholism Treatment Quarterly*, Volume 6, Number 1 1989.

The Haworth Press, Inc., 10 Alice Street, Binghamton, NY 13904-1580
EUROSPAN/Haworth, 3 Henrietta Street, London WC2E 8LU England

Library of Congress Cataloging-in-Publication Data

Co-dependency: issues in treatment and recovery / Bruce Carruth, Warner Mendenhall, editors.
    p.   cm.
  "Has also been published as Alcoholism treatment quarterly, volume 6, number 1, 1989" — T.p. verso.
  Includes bibliographies.
  ISBN 0-86656-920-0. — ISBN 0-86656-942-1 (pbk.)
  1. Co-dependence (Psychology) I. Carruth, Bruce. II. Mendenhall, Warner.
  [DNLM: 1. Alcoholism — Rehabilitation. 2. Family. 3. Substance Dependence — rehabilitation. W1 AL3147 v. 6 no. 1 / WM 274 C669]
RC569.5.C63C63   1989
616.86 — dc19
DNLM/DLC
for Library of Congress   89-1998
                                      CIP

Co-dependency:
Issues in Treatment and Recovery

CONTENTS

Introduction

Co-dependency has become the "hot" issue of the chemical dependency field of the late 1980s. Self-help books abound for people who define themselves as co-dependent. There are national and regional conferences for "ACOAs And Others Who Identify." Chemical dependency treatment facilities offer week long and month long residential treatment programs for the "resistant co-dependent." Where does it end? Where did it begin? What is a "co-dependent" anyway?

There is a remarkable amount of knowledge about co-dependency in print. The majority of this material is on the dynamics of co-dependency and is addressed to the consumer, the co-dependent individual. Less work has been done addressing the needs of counselors and therapists for "how to" information on diagnosis and treatment of individuals, couples and families. This monograph seeks to synthesize some of the existing knowledge and put that information in a context that will be useful in day-to-day treatment.

The eleven papers in this volume represent some remarkable insights from practicing therapists who work intensively with chemically dependent family systems. You will probably recognize the names of many of the authors as leaders in the emerging field of co-dependency treatment. These manuscripts represent their accumulated experience as clinicians as well as theoreticians.

We hope the ideas and skills presented here are useful in your practice.

Bruce Carruth, PhD

1

Co-dependency Definitions and Dynamics

Warner Mendenhall, PhD

The entire alcoholism field continues to struggle with language. For instance, in the fall of 1983 an article appeared in *Newsweek* entitled "Jellinek's Disease." General reading of Claudia Black, Janet Woititz, the Johnston Institute publications and other established sources leaves us with some confusion about the terms "co-dependent," "co-alcoholic," "para alcoholic." We need some agreement on the terms. Certainly, we don't need three words for one concept, yet all three of these words have been used to refer to any person, spouse, parent, child or grandparent who lives in a committed relationship with an alcoholic.

In choosing a word to carry an idea, we must be conscious of two things: first, we must use a word whose meaning reflects the concept; and second, we must use a word that accomplishes our purposes for meaning among those who hear. We must be careful, for with the word goes the structure of our thought and with the structure of our thought goes behavior. We are trying as professionals to change behavior from inebriation to sobriety, from stress to serenity. Therefore, I urge that we choose a vocabulary for our health field that not only meets the needs of the professionals to talk to each other but also meets the needs of the patient. Everyone in this field knows how hard it is to get a person to accept the label of "alcoholic" and the diagnosis of alcoholism. In fact, in our field we still hear among counselors the term "the disease concept" of alcoholism. It is not a "disease concept"; it is a disease. We in the field must take the leadership because the evidence is beyond dis-

---

Warner Mendenhall is Professor, Wayne College, University of Akron, Akron, OH, and is in psychotherapy practice in Canton, OH.

3

pute that chemical dependencies are psychosocial biogenetic diseases, no longer a concept, but a precept.

The fact that alcoholism is tragically and fundamentally misunderstood rests in myth deeply rooted in the ethical codes of the past. The most recent survey indicates that most people continue to hold tightly to the view that alcoholism is a shameful weakness. Unlike the hunchback, the heart patient, the diabetic, the epileptic, who are victims of a disease over which they have no control (i.e., they are seen as victims of their disability), the alcoholic is considered the cause of his/her disease. This idea has persisted from the beginning of the Christian Era to the present. The Roman philosopher Seneca said in 63 A.D., "Drunkenness is nothing but a condition of insanity purposely assumed."

The myths and misconceptions surrounding the disease must be rooted out regardless of the source, but in the meantime we must choose the language for our field that will help people get well.

Therefore, let me make a couple of suggestions about our language.

The prefix "co" has four meanings. I will not go into great length, but at least let me give you the flavor of each. First, "co" means "with," "together," "joint," "jointly," "mutual," "mutually." The second meaning is "in" or "to the same degree." The third meaning is "fellow," "partner," or "alternate"; and the final meaning of "co" is "operating together."

Based on the general focus of these meanings, the term "co-alcoholic" should refer to a person who is also suffering from the disease of alcoholism and not to the person who is living in a relationship to an alcoholic. Some therapists have failed to make this careful distinction and use the terms co-alcoholic to identify a non-alcoholic spouse. Such usage is clearly confusing—the term "co-alcoholic" should be reserved for the family member who is also alcoholic.

You see, what is shared is not the disease, but a dependency. Let's get a clearer conception of the term "dependency" before we move on and decide what to call family members. Again, the dictionary states that dependency means something that is dependent or is dependent upon something else—unfortunately another dictionary definition in which the definition of the term uses the term itself. So we must look further to our understanding of the word "depend": (1) to be contingent, (2) to require something as a necessary condition, (3) to have connection as a subordinate, (4) to hope often without alternate resources. And so dependency means (1) the quality of being conditional upon something else, (2) being subject to or subservient to, (3) something upon which one relies as object of one's trust. It is clear that dependency rather than alcoholism is the common connection or reality for the alcoholic and the family member. What is shared is dependency, not alcoholism.

This distinction suggests that we go further and re-examine a third term — "family disease." Alcoholism is not a family disease. One or two members of a family may have the disease, but clearly it is a disease that attacks us as individuals, not as families. We confuse the issue, blur the definition of disease, and distort the problems of family members by using the label "family disease." The disease is individual, not collective, so let's stop talking about the family "disease" and begin to say exactly what is meant: that people who live with a person with the disease develop problems. Let us honor the realness of those problems, let us honor the seriousness of what happens to these people by separating them from alcoholism and be willing to define their condition in terms that more closely identify their living reality. We have an alcoholic, or maybe two alcoholics in a family; then we have other suffering people who are not alcoholics. Let's get the proper labels and stop talking about some genre term "family disease." The fact that family members are affected by alcoholism does not make them co-alcoholics nor does it define a family disease. Have you ever heard of any other family disease? What a distortion of the reality. No wonder the public and our patients are confused: no wonder legislative policy is oblique and unclear.

Let's return to the notion of dependency as the functional link between family members. Dependency means being dependent upon something else: the alcoholic is dependent upon alcohol, and other family members are dependent on the alcoholic. The notions of "subordinate," "subservient," and "contingent" seem to fit well and to, in part, describe the person who lives with an alcoholic.

So let us proceed with the understanding that we will abandon the notion of the term "family disease" because it is a distortion of reality and because it is misleading in the public domain. Let us proceed by specifying the word "co-alcoholic" as a person in a committed relationship, usually a spouse who also suffers from the disease of alcoholism. And let us proceed for now and use the term "co-dependent" to describe the person living in a committed relationship with an alcoholic, but who is not suffering from the disease. If it is true, as we have heard it said, that the co-dependent is sicker than the chemically dependent person, we better start asking questions, doing research and reporting it in our journals so we can begin to treat these problems.

I define co-dependency as a primary condition that results from the debilitating physiological stress produced by living in a committed relationship with an alcoholic or drug dependent person.

Obviously, spouses and children are the most frequently available persons in the family pattern to be affected by this stress. With one in seven Americans genetically susceptible to alcoholism, the problem of co-dependency is ubiquitous indeed and demands our undivided attention. The primary interactional pattern in families suffering from addictive disease is inconsistency. The consequence of this inconsistency is that family members become afraid to express their feelings. It is well established that all form has feeling and if the path to experiencing feeling is blocked by the prohibitions or needs of the parent or by pre-occupation and inconsistency, the feelings cannot be experienced at the level of intrapsychic reality. What is not experienced must be acted out and this frequently brings destruction to others or self or both.

Another way to describe the family members' response is to say that in order to survive, they must repress their self-awareness, which means that these individuals do not get their needs met or feelings acknowledged. For co-dependent children especially, the only choice is a permanent destruction of self. The children are faced daily with abuse and frightening forms of behavior but are forbidden to articulate their fears. The greater damage is not caused by the trauma itself, but the repressed, hopeless despair over not being allowed to give expression to what one has suffered. It is not the suffering per se but the repression of the reality that constitutes the basis for the multigeneration continuation of this family distress. It is not being allowed to know what they know that makes these children of trauma. The co-dependent parent often requires the child to be good and forget the cruelty of the chemically dependent person. The child must comply because a loving parent is making the request; but underneath the compliance is deep humiliation, intimidation, destruction of dignity, loss of power and torment. Of course, many of these parents have been co-dependent since their own childhood and out of their repression of awareness, they attempt to normalize the dysfunction in order to stay in their relationship. The parent tries to hide their own impaired individuation process, but what the parent tries to hide will occupy the child the most. From this, children often believe they must rescue their parent so they can finally become the parent to them whom they needed from the beginning. This can, and often does, become a full-time occupation lasting throughout adult life and perhaps being transferred to other relationships.

This lifestyle of constant jeopardy and challenge to one's self-awareness (feelings and needs) leads to grandiose behavior as a way of preventing emergence of repressed material, humiliation and helplessness. Frequently, this behavior will be manifest in mistreatment of self or others. Suicide, murder, prejudice and war can all be explained as logical outcomes of childhood matters which are not childish matters.

On the rare occasion when a co-dependent parent has not also been co-dependent from childhood, the same dynamic of inconsistency leads to the same destruction of the self and a fear of depravation. As the family dominated by the inconsistency of chemical abuse continues, the spouse is blocked from their own needs and feelings and acquires a feeling of depravation which again must be normalized in order to maintain the myth of family. In this atmosphere of inconsistency, the co-dependent spouse is deluded by the hope that the other person's good side will win out and that then they and other family members will be fine. In the worst cases, the co-dependent parent will choose permanent destruction as the only choice and deny their pain and identity so completely that they join with the inconsistent, aggressive, chemically dependent spouse. The old saying, if you cannot beat them, join them, is fulfilled. Furthermore, if the parent has come from a dependent family situation themselves they will generally act the same way toward their own children as they were treated in an attempt to prove that their parents behaved correctly toward them.

Depending on the age of the person, co-dependency has a different etiology. If this dysfunctional adaptation begins in childhood, the tragic error is that the child comes to believe they are responsible for their needs not getting met. The child is mentally incapable of living outside their ego-centered world; therefore, they conclude that they must be making a mistake in their behavior else they would be getting the consistent treatment they need from their parents. A child needs to cry out to have their needs met and if they are not responded to, they may become schizophrenic or homicidal; but most often they get by through denial and repression of the pain of not getting their needs met. By the age of three, the child has experienced reject of refueling needs as well and senses that if the parent is not taken care of, he/she may die or go away. So the message to the child is—it is time to grow up now in order to keep the parent going and the symbiotic switch is complete. The child comes to depend on the thinking structure in an effort to take care of mom at the expense of developing their own feelings. The child rejects his/her needs and autonomy because the parent is so important to their survival. Growing up then becomes learning not to have needs and to erect a block between the thinking and feelings domains. The resulting message is—it is unsafe to be you.

For the young adult who gets involved in an alcoholic marriage, the genesis is different because this person has at least gained autonomy and has connected thoughts and feelings as a normal part of life. The co-dependency dysfunction begins as an act of love. Slowly, at first, the spouse begins to realize that he/she needs to accept the drinking pattern as normal and respond in a normal way by using culturally acceptable methods of problem resolution. The co-dependent acts to reduce the pain of his/her spouse, to ease the crisis by postponing his/her reaction and begin to protect other family members from the problem. The co-dependent's caretaking actually deprives the alcoholic of a learning experience that would bring awareness that alcohol is creating a problem. Clearly, the co-dependent is surprised and mystified by the failure of his/her efforts to bring relief for the problem.

Actually, they begin to help out a dysfunctional family member, believing that it is short term, committed to extra effort and work until the family member is back on their feet. Of course, this does not happen in an addictive family system, but the co-dependent response is to try harder, often more desperately, to be supportive, helpful and protective. The response by the co-dependent to this abnormal situation is to develop a coping mechanism for survival. The co-dependent simply cannot get a handle on what is going on — what they feel is consistently being denied by the spouse. The response is to separate their world into a private feeling world and a public behaving world. So just like the child, the adult learns that their behavior cannot be based on his/her feelings, but rather on the behavioral expectation of others. With this perspective in mind, let us examine the current research in the field of co-dependency.

There have been three perspectives used to examine the problem of co-dependency. One set of studies has tried to identify personality traits which increase the probability that individuals will select alcoholic or pre-alcoholic mates and then nurture their partners' tendency toward alcohol misuse. A second set of studies has focused on the stress created by being married to an alcoholic partner and has suggested that such spouse-characteristics as depression, anxiety, complaints of physical symptoms and poor health are a deviate result of this stress. A third set of studies has described alternative ways in which spouses cope with their alcoholic partners and establish satisfactory lifestyles even though they are enmeshed in disturbed marriages.

The first perspective assumes that the alcoholic's spouse suffers from long-standing personality deficiency, while the second contends that they are essentially normal people who show the effects of being under intermittent stress. The third perspective argues that many spouses can cope adequately with the stress they experience and lead essentially normal lives.

With three exceptions, all the research on spouses of alcoholics has been done on women. This research has been less than conclusive and is strewn with structural errors in research design and interpretation of data. Specifically, samples have been self-selected and unrepresentative and have not been matched with control groups.

One notable exception is the research done under an NIAAA

grant by Rudolf Moos, John Finny and Wendy Gamble published in *Journal of Studies of Alcohol*, Vol. 43, No. 9, 1982.

First, and contrary to some earlier descriptive studies, Moos et al. found no difference based on gender: husbands of women patients and wives of men patients reported no difference on the seven sets of variables and so this research combines the genders in reporting the results.

Essentially, the research focus is on three questions: (1) Do the spouses of recovered (their term) alcoholic patients function as well as the spouses of their non-alcoholic community neighbors? (2) Do the spouses of relapsed patients function more poorly than those of recovered patients and of community controls and if so, in what areas? (3) Can a general framework that incorporates such factors as partner characteristics, life change events and coping responses contribute to a better understanding of functioning among spouses of alcoholics and normal controls?

There were only three differences between the spouses of recovered alcoholic patients and those of community controls. The spouses of the recovered alcoholics were less likely to have drunk alcohol during the past month, and they reported fewer social contacts and less emphasis on an active-recreational orientation in their families. In conjunction with the recovered patients functioning about as well as their non-alcoholic community counterparts, these findings show that some recovered alcoholics and their spouses can attain essentially normal functioning.

In comparison with the controls, the spouses of relapsed alcoholics drank more alcohol, experienced more negative life events, participated in fewer social activities, and enjoyed less cohesion and active recreation in their family environments. Furthermore, the spouses of currently heavy drinking alcoholics also experienced more drinking problems, depression and medical conditions, and tended to change jobs and visit doctors more frequently.

In corroboration of previous research, the overall results indicate that individuals suffer some stress effects from living with an alcoholic partner but that these effects diminish when the partner makes an effort to control his or her excessive drinking. Spouses of active alcoholic partners complained of more anxiety, depression, and physical symptoms and reported visiting doctors more frequently.

Therefore, the results provide no support for the hypothesis that, relative to spouses of controls, spouses of alcoholics are more likely to suffer from disturbed personalities. Nor is there support for the idea that their functioning is detrimentally affected by their partners' successful control of alcohol misuse. Although spouses of recovered alcoholics complained of some depression, anxiety, and physical symptoms, their complaints were no more serious than those of spouses of community controls. The most parsimonious conclusion is that spouses of alcoholics are basically normal people who are trying to cope with disturbed marriages and behaviorally dysfunctional partners. Previous findings supporting the personality and decompensation hypotheses may be due to many of the spouses having been in crisis situations, having sought help for themselves, and not having been compared with adequately matched controls.

The author's findings are consistent with the stress and coping perspectives. Spouses who are under more stress because their alcoholic partners are drinking heavily experience more mood and health-related dysfunction than spouses of controls or of recovered alcoholics. Furthermore, spouses are affected by their partners' other characteristics (such as mood and physical symptoms) as well as by stressful life-change events (such as loss of income and legal problems) that may be related to the partners' drinking problem. These results indicate that complaints of depression and health-related problems among spouses of abstinent alcoholics do not necessarily provide support for the disturbed personality hypothesis since such spouses may experience high levels of stress due to their partners' continuing dysfunction in other areas.

Based on this evidence, a central concern of treatment is concern with stress. First then, some myths about stress.

Hans Selye, MD, suggests in his seminal work in this field *The Stress of Life*, 1963, that:

1. It is not simple nervous tension.
2. It is not an emergency discharge of hormones from the adrenal medullas.
3. It is not everything that causes secretion of ACTH.
4. It is not always the nonspecific result of damage.
5. It is not the same as a deviation from homeostasis.

6. It is not anything that causes an alarm reaction.
7. It is not identified with alarm reaction.
8. It is not a nonspecific reaction.
9. It is not a specific reaction.
10. It is not necessarily bad.
11. Stress cannot and should not be avoided.

Stress is, therefore, the nonspecific response of the body to any demand whether it is caused by, or results in, pleasant or unpleasant conditions. In all conditions we know that certain things happen in the body.

In the presence of stress, there is:

1. adrenocortical enlargement.
2. atrophy of the thymicolymphatic organs.
3. gastrointestinal ulcers.
4. loss of body weight.
5. derangement in body temperature.
6. disappearance of eosinophil cells and other chemical alterations.
7. inflammation — to the extent that general inflammation prevents local stresses — this suggests a limit to stress reaction response.

And that limit to stress response turns out to be very important. (See Figure 1.)

1. First response is for the systems to fall below normal.
2. Then through adaptation gain reaction, and capacity rises above normal.
3. But eventually exhaustion and resistance drops below normal.

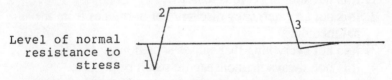

Level of normal
resistance to
stress

FIGURE 1

There is adaptability but eventually it runs out: the amount of resistance coping mechanisms is finite. We cannot go on resisting stress indefinitely.

The other instructive notion from Selye is that if one stays under stress too long, one cannot return to the normal and thereby lives in an impaired state — impaired and not able to adapt to the next stress (i.e., the gain in resistive capacity above normal is less). (See Figure 2.)

Most people and some clinicians believe that after being exposed to stress or stress activity, a rest can restore a person to where they were before; this is false. It is the restoration of the superficial adaptation energy from the deep reserves that tricks us into believing that the loss has been made good, but the reserves are gradually depleted. Co-dependents have had their reserve depleted, never again able to marshall the adaptive response to the degree they once could. Recovery for the co-dependent usually is less complete than the alcoholic because of this depletion. I am sure you have heard it said that the co-dependent is sicker than the alcoholic. We need to recognize that this is based in fact.

> Stress is like the wind.
> Who has seen the wind?
> Neither you nor I.
> But when the trees bow down their heads,
> The wind is passing by.

And so our patients come with bowed head. Selye has suggested some helpful guidelines for all of us:

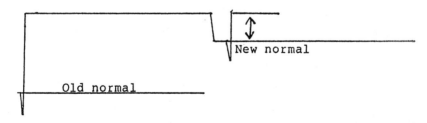

FIGURE 2

1. *Find your own natural stress level*. People differ with regard to the amount and kind of work they consider worth doing to meet the exigencies of daily life and to assure their future security and happiness. In this respect, all of us are influenced by hereditary predispositions and the expectations of our society. Only through planned self-analysis can we establish what we really want; too many people suffer all their lives because they are too conservative to risk a radical change and break with traditions.
2. *Altruistic egoism*. The selfish hoarding of the goodwill, respect, esteem, support, and love of our neighbor is the most efficient way to give vent to our pent-up energy and to create enjoyable, beautiful, or useful things. Just accept a compliment or praise.
3. *Earn thy neighbor's love*. This motto, unlike love on command, is compatible with man's natural structure and, although it is based on altruistic egoism, it could hardly be attacked as unethical. Who would blame anyone who wants to assure his own homeostasis and happiness by accumulating the treasure of other people's benevolence towards him? Yet, this makes him virtually unassailable, for nobody wants to attack and destroy those upon whom he/she depends.

We need to build on this beginning to find the most helpful therapy for those whose stress adaptation has been mortally wounded and whose responses will remain impaired.

Let's once again remind ourselves of just what co-dependency really is—an addiction. Psychological writers frequently list ten addictions—addiction to food, sugar, alcohol, drugs, money, caffeine, nicotine, sex, work, and relationships. It is within this last area where we find co-dependency, a set of symptoms that is characterized by chronic neglect of the self in favor of someone else. Co-dependency addiction keeps people away from their own experience. It prevents them from knowing what they feel. By the time we see these people in our offices, they have learned to adjust, to survive by destroying their emotion—sometimes they even think they are getting better because they confuse getting better with feeling better. For instance, one patient followed his friend home to a town fifty miles away just to be sure she got home safe and did not get a DWI. What could he have done about either following at a half-mile distance? He felt better that she was safe that night, but he was not getting better for he was consumed by her needs.

By the time they get to our clinic co-dependents are removed from reality, no longer have a coherent thought process, are removed from their own experience having become dishonest about their experiences in order to survive. They have learned to adjust to destructive situations, learned to ignore their intuitions, begun to feel like a victim, are void of creative responses to life, are not dead and yet not alive and destroyed spiritually. These patients have a limited awareness of themselves and are vague about the nature of their problems.

Remember that this process begins with good motives — worrying about someone they love. But co-dependents begin to think that there is something wrong with them because the other person's behavior is not changing. Some have suffered from the illusion that they are powerful enough to make another person (the alcoholic) change. The co-dependent addiction comes to the point of being focused outward and missing the self: trying to control, trying to decide how they can make happen what they want to happen. They come to plan life around another and then dictate how they want the other person to be centered on them like they are centered on the other.

These dynamics of co-dependency can be summarized as follows:

1. Co-dependents are out of touch with their own experience because they are, or have been, in a pathological relationship with a mood altering experience — living with a chemically dependent person — which leads to the neglect of children, work, friends, and most importantly, self. As one co-dependent succinctly stated, "Our being becomes rooted in their being and we become strangers to ourselves."

2. This neglect means that feelings are discounted. Co-dependents don't know that they have a right to feelings and in fact learn not to know feelings. In most chemically-dependent families there is no feedback because there is no talking about important things.

At best feelings come out "through the cracks," transferred to another person.

3. Co-dependents are always in emotional pain and pain becomes the norm — a norm of despair and hopelessness about getting needs met. They never get what they need from someone who is in a relationship with a chemical.

4. Co-dependents learn not to ask for help, so they come to handle everything in order to survive. The sense of weakness that comes from being dependent only on oneself, especially if you are a child, without the wisdom or the help of others who have shared the same experience is overwhelming. There is no wisdom because what works in one situation is not generally able to work in other situations when one is living with a chemically dependent person because the only consistent feature is inconsistency.

5. Co-dependents not only do not get their needs met, they come to be unable even to identify their needs. One thing is clear: other people's needs are always greater then theirs.

6. Co-dependents, like the public, are often fooled by the alcoholic marriage. Specifically, co-dependents mistake intensity for intimacy, obsession for care, and control for security.

7. Co-dependents come to have an extremely high tolerance for inappropriate behavior.

8. Co-dependents come to feel terrible because they have anger toward another person which must be suppressed. They don't even dare yell at the alcoholic, and if people cannot be angry, then they have no choice: they are trapped, they become victims.

9. Co-dependents do not recognize what has happened to their own health. It is hard for co-dependents to know that they are at risk. It is hard for co-dependents to commit to solving their problem because co-dependents come self-righteously to believe that the alcoholic has the problem. The co-dependent has massive, sincere delusion.

10. Co-dependents have learned to adjust, but they have not learned how to change.

11. Co-dependents are compulsive about pretending. For instance, the co-dependent never tells the truth, never really names what is going on. The co-dependent pretends that reality is not real.

12. Co-dependency is a condition of reactivity: all behaviors are

done in response to another's behavior, nothing is pro-active or spontaneous.

13. Co-dependents get defensive trying to control their feelings, and in alcoholic families feelings in general are kept down and specific feelings are discouraged.

14. Co-dependents are isolated from self and others and as a result, there is a loss of reality checks; the loss of how to tell what is real.

15. By the time we see these patients in our office, usually the pain is so intense that there is constant tension in their lives. At best, co-dependents feel that they are nothing more than the sum of others' expectations.

16. The process of co-dependency is contagious: others get easily pulled into the system because people try to help and try to understand. However, the result is that co-dependents have support groups that tell them to stay stuck.

17. By the time co-dependents come for help, they have failed — tried harder — failed — tried harder — so many times that they feel hopeless and helpless. Their unsuccessful coping skills have become a ritual of compulsivity, despair, and preoccupation; and when nothing works, co-dependents become convinced that something is lacking in them, a sense of grandiosity about their inadequacy.

18. The sense of loss about the relationship, the sense of loss of loving, the sense of loss about the future, the sense of loss about self, leaves co-dependents feeling that they have violated their personal goals and standards of self-expectation.

19. Out of this reality comes a belief system in the co-dependent that leads to impaired thinking, compulsive behavior and a feeling of unmanageability. For instance, denial, protectiveness, embarrassment (don't tell, keep it in the family), guilt (if I were better), doing it all, worry as a way of life, fear, lying, false hope, confusion, sex hopelessness, anger over concern of self or grandiosity.

There is, of course, much more that we could do on the topics already covered and, of course, many other possible topics; but such concerns must be examined at another time. Here I have pleaded for a language of wellness, explained the role of stress, and examined the major dynamics of co-dependency.

Co-dependence:
Our Most Common Addiction—
Some Physical, Mental, Emotional
and Spiritual Perspectives

Charles L. Whitfield, MD

Co-dependence is a disease of lost selfhood. I define it as *any suffering and/or dysfunction that is associated with or results from focusing on the needs and behavior of others*. Co-dependents become so focused upon or pre-occupied with important and even less important people in their lives that they neglect their true self—who they really are. As Schaef[21] says, it leads to a process of "nonliving," which is progressive.

I list below seven recent definitions of co-dependence and synthesize what these have in common in my overall definition above.

SOME DEFINITIONS OF CO-DEPENDENCE

(1) . . . an exaggerated dependent pattern of learned behaviors, beliefs and feelings that make life painful. It is a dependence on people and things outside the self, along with neglect of the self to the point of having little self identity.

(Smalley, S: cited in Wegscheider-Cruse, 1985)

(2) . . . preoccupation and extreme dependence (emotionally, socially, and sometimes physically) on a person or object. Eventually, this dependence on another person becomes a pathological condition that affects the co-dependent in all other relationships. This may include . . . all persons who (1) are in a love or marriage relationship with an alcoholic; (2) have one or more alcoholic par-

ents or grandparents; or (3) grew up in an emotionally repressive family. . . . It is a primary disease and a disease within every member of an alcoholic family.

(Wegscheider-Cruse, 1985)

(3) . . . ill health, maladaptive or problematic behavior that is associated with living with, working with or otherwise being close to a person with alcoholism (other chemical dependence or other chronic impairment). It affects not only individuals, but families, communities, businesses, and other institutions, and even whole societies.

(Whitfield, 1984, 1986)

(4) . . . an emotional, psychological, and behavioral pattern of coping that develops as a result of an individual's prolonged exposure to, and practice of, a set of oppressive rules — rules which prevent the open expression of feeling, as well as the direct discussion of personal and interpersonal problems.

(Subby, 1984, 1987)

(5) . . . a personality disorder based on: a need to control in the face of serious adverse consequences; neglecting one's own needs; boundary distortions around intimacy and separation; enmeshment with certain dysfunctional people; and other manifestations such as denial, constricted feelings, depression, and stress-related medical illness. (paraphrased from Cermak)

(Cermak, 1986)

(6) . . . a stress-induced preoccupation with another's life, leading to maladaptive behavior.

(Mendenhall, 1987)

(7) . . . a disease that has many forms and expression and that grows out of a disease process that. . . . I call the addictive process . . . the addictive process is an unhealthy and abnormal disease process whose assumptions, beliefs, and lack of spiritual awareness lead to a process of nonliving which is progressive . . .

(Schaef, 1986)

Endemic in ordinary humankind, co-dependence can mimic, be associated with, aggravate, and even lead to many of the conditions—physical, mental, emotional, or spiritual—that befall us. It develops from turning our responsibility for our life and happiness over to our ego and to other people.

Co-dependence is the most common addiction people develop. It comes from focusing so much outside of ourselves, that we lose touch with what is inside of us. Inside are our internal cues that assist us in countless ways: our feelings, sensations, sensibilities, intuitions, and some of our physical functioning, such as heart rate and respiratory rate. These and more are part of an exquisite feedback system that we can call our *inner life*. Our inner life is a major part of our consciousness. And our consciousness is who we are—our true self.

There is nothing harmful or wrong with looking outside of ourself. In fact, doing so is useful not only in everyday life, but in our survival. However, co-dependents overdo it by focusing outward so much that they neglect their inner lives to an extent that they suffer inordinately and unnecessarily. This suffering often leads to dysfunction.

The following illustrates some characteristics of experiences, states and dynamics that may develop in an advanced stage of co-dependence

SOME CHARACTERISTICS OF CO-DEPENDENCE

My good feelings about who I am stem from being liked by you and receiving approval from you.

Your struggles affect my serenity. My mental attention focuses on solving your problems or relieving your pain.

My mental attention is focused on pleasing you, protecting you, manipulating you to "do it my way."

My self-esteem is bolstered by solving your problems and relieving your pain.

My own hobbies and interests are put aside. My time is spent sharing your interests and hobbies.

Because I feel you are a reflection of me, your clothing and personal appearance are dictated by my desires.

Your behavior is dictated by my desires.
I am not aware of how I feel. I am aware of how *you* feel.
I am not aware of what I want. I ask you what *you* want.
If I am not aware of something, I *assume*.
The dreams I have for my future are linked to you.
My fear of your anger and rejection determine what I say or do.
In our relationship I use giving as a way of feeling safe.
As I involve myself with you, my social circle diminishes.
To connect with you, I put my values aside.
I value your opinion and way of doing things more than my own.
The quality of my life depends on the quality of yours.

Author unknown
Circulated by Co-Dependents Anonymous[8]

Co-dependence is *addiction to looking elsewhere*. We believe that something outside of ourself—i.e., outside of our true self—can give us happiness and fulfillment. But has it ever done so in any lasting way? Whether the "elsewhere" is people, places, things, behaviors, or other experiences, we neglect our own self for it, so that we get a payoff of some sort from focusing outward. The pay-off is most often a reduction in painful feelings, although it may at times be a *temporary* increase in joyful feelings. But this feeling or *mood alteration* is predicated principally upon the other, and not on our wants and needs, not based upon our own internal cues.

What we need is a healthy balance of awareness of our inner life and our outer life. This balance has nothing to do with "normal," "proper," or "required." Rather, it has to do with *what is*, what is happening precisely in the eternal now of our own individual con- sciousness. To have such a healthy balance does not come automat- ically, given our current world where nearly everyone is co-depen- dent most of the time. In fact, we learn to be co-dependent from others around us. It is in this sense a *contagious* or acquired illness. From the time we are born, it is modeled and taught to us by a seemingly endless string of important people in our life: parents, teachers, siblings, friends, heroes and heroines. Co-dependence is reinforced by the media, government, organized religion, and the helping professions.

As I have developed in *Healing the Child Within*, co-dependence comes from our trying to protect our delicate true self (child within) from what may appear to be insurmountable forces outside ourselves.[28] But our true self is a paradox. Not only is it sensitive, delicate, and vulnerable — but it is also powerful. In fact, it is so powerful, that in a *full recovery program* for co-dependence, it heals through a process of self-responsibility and creativity which is often awesome to behold.

When our alive true self goes into hiding, in order to please its parent figures and thus to survive, a false, co-dependent self emerges to take its place. We thus lose our awareness of our true self to such an extent that we *lose awareness of its existence.* We lost contact with who we really are. Gradually, we begin to get used to that false self. Then it becomes a habit, and finally an addiction.

Co-dependence is not only the most common addiction, it is the base out of which all our addictions and compulsions emerge. Underneath nearly every addiction and compulsion lies co-dependence. And what runs them is a sense of shame that our true self, our child within, is somehow defective or inadequate, combined with the innate and healthy drive of our true self to realize and express itself. Whichever form it may take, the addiction or compulsion becomes the manifestation of the erroneous notion that something outside ourself can make us happy and fulfilled.

Like any addiction/compulsion, co-dependence is giving away our power, although when we do that, we are not usually conscious of it. Then how does it come about? While we can become co-dependent any time in our life, most of us learn it from birth.

NATURAL HISTORY OF CO-DEPENDENCE

When we get into conflict or experience a loss, we hurt. Impactful others do not support or allow us to heal our hurt, and so we stuff it. The genesis of co-dependence begins by the *repression* of our *inner life*: our observations, feelings, and reactions. Often our parents, and then others, and eventually *we* begin to *invalidate* these, our often crucial *internal cues*.

Because we focus so much on the needs of others, we begin to neglect our own needs, and by so doing we stifle our true self, our child within. Usually early in this process we begin to deny a family secret or another secret. Such secrets are often so charged with painful feelings—also part of our true self—that we have to push them down into our subconscious mind.

But we still have feelings, often of hurt. Since we continue to stuff our feelings, we become increasingly tolerant of emotional pain. We often become numb. And because we stuff our feelings, we are unable to grieve our everyday losses to completion.

To survive, we begin to construct a false or co-dependent self. All of the above blocks our growth and development in the mental, emotional and spiritual aspects of our being. But we have a strong desire to contact and know our true self. We learn that "quick fixes," such as compulsive behaviors, will allow us to glimpse our true self and, by letting some feelings emerge, will let off some of the tension. However, if the compulsive behavior is destructive to us or to others, we may feel shame and a resulting lower self-esteem. At this point we may begin to feel more and more out of control and we try to compensate by the need to control even more. We may end up deluded and hurt, and often project our pain onto others.

We continue alienated from our true self. Our tension has now built to such an extent that we may develop stress-related illness manifested by aches and pains, and often by dysfunction of one or more body organs. We are now in an advanced state of co-dependence, and may progressively deteriorate so that we experience one or more of: extreme mood swings, difficulty with intimate relationships, and chronic unhappiness. For those who are attempting to recover from alcoholism, another chemical dependence, or another condition or illness, this advanced state of co-dependence may seriously interfere.

The development or genesis of co-dependence may thus be summarized as follows.

Genesis of Co-dependence

1. Invalidation and repression of our inner life's internal cues, such as our observations, feelings and reactions
2. Neglecting our needs
3. Beginning to stifle our true self (child within)

4. Beginning to construct our co-dependent (false) self
5. Denying a family or other secret
6. Increasing tolerance of and numbness to emotional pain
7. Inability to grieve a loss to completion
8. Blocking of growth (mental, emotional, spiritual)
9. Compulsive behaviors in order to lessen pain and to glimpse our true self
10. Progressive shame and loss of self-esteem
11. Feeling out of control. Need to control more
12. Delusion and projection of pain
13. Stress-related illness develops
14. Compulsions worsen
15. Progressive deterioration

- Extreme mood swings
- Difficulty with intimate relationships
- Chronic unhappiness
- Interference with recovery from alcoholism/CD and other conditions

Whether we are an infant or a child growing up with such a co-dependent person, or whether we are an adult living with or close to them, it is highly likely that with our present awareness and coping skills we will be negatively affected. By the process described in this issue and elsewhere[12,14,28] our true self will be stifled. We focus on others as a survival tool, to stop the hurting and to help our lives work better in the short run. However, it doesn't work well, and persistently doing so develops into co-dependence.

PHYSICAL ILLNESS FROM CO-DEPENDENCE

Somewhere from the middle to an advanced stage of co-dependence, physical illness may develop. One possible way that it may develop is by the dynamic of stress that is unhandled to such an extent that it becomes *distress*, which then often develops into stress-related illness. Most of medical practice is spent treating stress-related illnesses of all sorts.[11,24,29] In an attempt to avoid the pain of short-term stress or "eustress," that which is usually easier to deal with, co-dependents stuff their feelings and attempt to please others. Such avoidance usually ends up producing long-term stress, which we call distress.

Another way that physical illness may develop, and likely intimately related to the stress model, is that of disallowed or repressed grieving. From birth we are taught dysfunctional family rules, the incorporation of which is part of the genesis of co-dependence. Some of these rules include: (1) it's not OK to talk about problems or to talk about or express our feelings openly, (2) communicate indirectly—through another person than the one you need to talk to, (3) don't be selfish, (4) always be strong, good, perfect, and happy, (5) it's *not* OK to be playful, and (6) don't rock the boat.[23] These rules may serve to protect us from short-term conflict and pain, but they set the stage for hiding our true self, including its needs, wants and feelings.

With the inevitable repeated losses in our lives, these rules tend to prevent us from grieving our losses in a healthy way. And what we do not *grieve* healthily, we tend to *act out* in physical, mental, emotional or behavioral ways, which are often problematic. For example, *anger* unexpressed and unprocessed may be manifest in numerous ways, including depression, compulsion, and addiction; family and child abuse; and possibly even a lowering of our body's immune response—which is a major factor in our ability to fight off infection and cancer.

Unexpressed *fear* can result in anxiety and panic disorders, insomnia, heart arrhythmias (abnormalities of the heart beat), sexual dysfunction, and other stress-related illness. Unexpressed *guilt* may lead to self-neglect, compulsion and addiction, other self-destructive behavior, and other chronic conditions. And unexpressed *shame* can result in self-neglect, compulsion and addiction, other self-destructive behavior, sexual dysfunction, and other chronic conditions. Our feelings are not just "mental" occurrences; they are complex *physiological* interactions within our sophisticated system of internal cues.[10,28,30]

Preliminary studies suggest that writing and sharing our feelings strengthens our body's immune response, as shown by the following scientific study. Twenty-five adults kept a diary of disturbing life events for five days, and wrote how they felt about each of them. Another twenty-five adults kept a diary about superficial life events only. When their immune response was measured at six weeks, and then six months later, as compared with their baseline, the former group had improved immune response, whereas the latter group had no change.[19] Studies like these, plus our clinical observations,[25] indicate that when we do not grieve in a healthy way, meaning that when we do not let our true self experience and express itself, we often get sick.[28]

In my medical practice, which for the first few years was mostly conventional somatically oriented medicine, and then the last fourteen years, which has been progressively psychotherapy, I have observed numerous co-dependent patients. I noticed a pattern of chronic functional, psychosomatic or physical illness in these people, covering a spectrum from asthma, to migraine headaches, to arthritis, to hearing loss, all of which tended to improve substantially or clear with treatment that was specific for their co-dependence.

I believe that the concept of co-dependence will in some important way eventually impact upon the practice of medicine, which includes psychiatry. Is it possible that co-dependence is a co-factor in the pathogenesis of cancer? How might co-dependence affect the development of cardiovascular diseases? And many other medical and surgical conditions, including AIDS? Others are writing on the important and often crucial effect of the mind and spirit on the body,[11,16,24] but none has related it to co-dependence.

PSYCHOLOGICAL ILLNESS

Since its beginning, the mental health field has been helping people with co-dependence. What is now changing are the ways we describe these people's conditions and help them recover. For awhile we used fancier descriptive terms like "passive aggressive," "locus of control," and "outer directed." And simpler ones like "victim," "martyr," and "stress." We helped these people get to know themselves better and take more responsibility for their lives. What is new and more helpful about co-dependence includes a reframing and broadening of the dynamics of the conditions that we were so long observing, and a more precise and sophisticated way of helping people who suffer from them.

Most of this article involves the genesis and effect of co-dependence upon our psychological functioning. We can now begin to explore and examine this involvement further. When we do, we discover that we may end up having more questions than satisfactory answers. Two questions: How does co-dependence impinge upon or fit in with the various psychological disorders? and, How useful will it be to describe co-dependence as an independent disorder or disease entity?

For those helping professionals who are aware of and treat people with co-dependence, describing it as a discreet disorder is useful. Whatever guise it may first present as, it is helpful to know that either as base or as associated in some important way, co-dependence is involved as causal in the person's difficulties or suffering. This is practical because co-dependence is such an imminently treatable condition. As described in this volume and elsewhere, there are effective treatment approaches and techniques available for co-dependence as a specific disorder. It is likely that these will be progressively refined with time and experience, and that we will create additional treatment approaches and techniques.

When we describe co-dependence as a specific disorder, how broad should our description be? And will it be most useful to fit it into a *category* of disorders? Cermak (1986) describes it under the category of personality disorders — specifically most like mixed personality disorder — and reviews general ways to treat it. Describing it as a personality disorder alone is simplistic and limiting, although such an approach has advantages and disadvantages. Advantages include having available discreet diagnostic criteria for those who may be less familiar with co-dependence. And by doing so, the diagnosis has potential to be more available to the general mental health professional, as well as the public. However, co-dependence appears to be not even close to being accepted by the mainstream of mental health. In fact, while awareness is growing slowly, most are not even aware of its existence. Co-dependence is so basic and so pervasive among humans that it likely affects not just most who come for some sort of psychotherapy or counseling, but effects *most people*.

Since co-dependence is not so far accepted as a diagnosis in our diagnostic code books such as DSM-III-R or ICD-9-CM, Insurance companies are not aware of its existence, and therefore will not pay for its treatment. So we have to find, from the patient or client's history, an acceptable additional diagnosis if they are to be considered for reimbursement for treatment, as they are entitled when they are covered by health insurance. While any disorder may be a manifestation of or associated with co-dependence, the following are frequently: avoidant personality disorder, dependent personality disorder, compulsive personality disorder, mixed personality disorder (now called personality disorder not otherwise specified), dysthymic disorder, anxiety disorder, and post traumatic stress disorder.

We can consider viewing co-dependence as both lying *within* a diagnostic category of e.g., personality disorders, and we can view it — and probably more accurately — as a general and pervasive part of the painful side of the human condition, such that it *is itself a category under which many, if not most, conditions can be subsumed.*

Personality disorders are said to be less treatable than other conditions. However, with a specific and full recovery program,[1,2,5,7,8,28,30] co-dependence is usually more treatable. While recovery is generally slow, an varies from person to person, when approached from the dynamic of co-dependence, the same person — who otherwise might have been diagnosed as having a personality disorder and therefore "less treatable" — would now have a greater chance for recovery, a better prognosis. The latter would depend, of course, on whether the therapist had specific training and skills in treating co-dependence *and* in recognizing and treating, or referring, other major and treatable psychological disorders.

Disadvantages of having co-dependence as a distinct diagnostic entity include that by so doing it may lose its power as a general and pervasive part of the painful side of the human condition,[22] and thus as a focal point from which we can begin to get free, to recover. Another is that because it is as much a category as a distinct disorder, there is the potential that counselors and therapists may diagnose it alone, and neglect or miss other important or treatable conditions.

Another concern is when "co-dependence" or "co-dependent" are used to describe a certain symptom, sign, behavior or dynamic, when it would be more appropriate, accurate, or helpful to use a more precise word, phrase or more elaborate description. This is one of the criticisms that some people make about these terms. There are other words in the mental health field that have been and are still being similarly misused, e.g., words such as "narcissistic," "schizophrenic," and "borderline."

SPIRITUAL ILLNESS

Spirituality has to do with our relationships. These include our relationship with our self, others, and the Universe (i.e., a Higher Power). As I have described in the first issue of *Alcoholism Treatment Quarterly*, and later elsewhere, spirituality has certain characteristics, such as its being: subtle, yet powerful, and thus paradoxical; personal, practical, and experiential; inclusive, supportive and nurturing, yet also transcending the physical and psychological realms of our existence.[29,31]

We learn to heal the woundedness of our true self, our child within, out of the constriction we feel from our co-dependent self. We learn and heal in three of our states of being: (1) when we are *alone, i.e., with our true self*, (2) with *others*, especially close others, and (3) with our *Higher Power*. These three states eventually merge at times as we heal.

William James described alcoholics as being "frustrated mystics." A mystic is someone who wants to experience everything fully, including non-ordinary realms of awareness or consciousness, and especially their relationship to God/Goddess/All-That-Is. I believe that co-dependent people are also frustrated mystics. (I have already mentioned that inside every alcoholic or other drug dependent person is a co-dependent. The same applies for adult children of alcoholic or other dysfunctional families.) Thus, rather than being simply an *escape* from reality, compulsion, addiction and co-addiction, i.e., co-dependence, is also a *search*. It starts out as a search for happiness and fulfillment outside ourself. And after repeated frustration of being unable to do so, it ultimately becomes a search for inner wholeness and completion.

One way to describe this spiritual journey, this search through both outer and inner in relationship, is to use a model from a modern book of spiritual or transpersonal psychology, a modern holy book that increasing numbers of recovering people are examining, called *A Course in Miracles*.⁹ The course describes the co-dependent or addicted relationship (which it calls a "Special Relationship") by at least ten characteristics. While the concept of the special relationship is complex and is spread throughout the Course, I list ten of its major characteristics below.

Special (Co-dependent) Relationship

1. Denies the need for relationship with or assistance from Higher Power.
2. Is based on self-hate from guilt and shame.
3. Hides this shame and guilt under the guise of love of another.
4. It thus places the answer to our shame/guilt outside of us.
5. It assumes that something is lacking in us and that we need it to be happy.
6. It fixes expectations on the other, i.e., the special relationship. By so doing, it denies the other's true Identity in Higher Power, i.e., that they are a part of God.
7. It is based on the scarcity principle, that there is only a limited amount of love to go around.
8. It becomes the focus of our anger and resentments.
9. It shifts responsibility for our happiness to the other, i.e., the special relationship. For example, "If only you were or would be such and such, then I would be happy."
10. The ego (false or co-dependent self) uses the special relationship for attacking the other by projecting our shame and guilt onto the other, and thus promising salvation, i.e., happiness and fulfillment.

I see this description and concept as an expansion of co-dependence as we have described it throughout this volume and as others have described it elsewhere. These characteristics are related to some of the core issues of co-dependence, such as denial, control, difficulty trusting, low self-esteem, difficulty handling conflict, and difficulty giving and receiving love.

When I first read these characteristics in the *Course* and in the writings of Ken Wapnick, who is its clearest interpreter,²⁶ I felt discouraged, and even hopeless. If most relationships are this way, how can relationships ever work? The *Course*'s answer to the special relationship is that *we do not have to control* more by being something we are not, e.g., by doing more, better or different, which the ego would egg us on to do. Rather, all we need is a "little willingness" to open to the healing power of God, which it refers to as the awareness of "love's presence," among other terms. When we do so, a miracle happens. We heal.

We simply shift our way of thinking. We change our mind about our mind. What results is a *process* that continues as the *Course*'s answer to the special relationship, which it calls the Holy Relationship. I summarize its characteristics as follows.

Holy (Healthy) Relationship

1. Based on my love of Higher Power, and true self/Higher Self.
2. I see this love in everyone.
3. I take responsibility for my suffering by looking within myself.
4. I address and release my shame, guilt, hurt, anger and resentment through the forgiveness process.
5. I realize that there is only abundance of Love, and that the scarcity principle is only an illusion.
6. I know that there is nothing lacking in me, that I am a perfect child of God, and that my natural state is Serenity.
7. I respect my positive ego and use it as an assistant in my growth.
8. I use daily spiritual practices.
9. I live and relate in the present moment, the Now.
10. In relationships I am open and communicating, trusting, gentle, peaceful, joyful and celebrating.

These characteristics are of a healthy relationship, which includes a balance of healthy dependence and healthy independence.[30] And they are compatible with Twelve Step programs and with the core teachings of the world's great religious systems, both Eastern and Western, including Christianity and Judaism. Ancient and modern spiritual teachers and literature say that to realize Serenity, we first have to discover who we are. The Second of the Twelve Steps says "Came to believe that a Power greater than ourselves could restore us to sanity," wherein sanity means wholeness or completeness. By so doing, we become progressively more aware of *all* parts of our Self, including our lower self (physical, mental, and emotional), our Heart (or acceptance through conflict) level — which is our true self, and is the bridge to our Higher Self (intuition, creativity, compassion and God consciousness). We thus have within each of us a Divine part, which means that Higher Power is in us, and that we are in Higher Power. Jesus said, "The kingdom of Heaven is within." When we so discover our Whole Self, we then begin to forgive it and love it. And when we have done so, we are free — we realize Serenity.[4,20,29,31]

TREATMENT OF CO-DEPENDENCE

The First Step of the fellowship of Co-Dependents Anonymous reads, "We admitted we were powerless over others — that our lives had become unmanageable." To treat and heal the suffering and dysfunction of co-dependence, we first realize that we are *powerless* over the others in our relationships. We are powerless over their beliefs, their thoughts, their feelings, their decisions and choices, and their behavior. But we discover we are *powerful* over ourselves, our own beliefs, thoughts, feelings, decisions, choices and behaviors. We begin to reclaim our personal power through a process of increasing *awareness* and by taking *responsibility* for our well-being and functioning. The formula I use is Power = Awareness plus Responsibility.

Since co-dependence is a disease of lost selfhood,[6,13,28] we can increase our awareness and responsibility by beginning to heal our true self. To rediscover our true self and heal our child within, we can begin a *process* that involves the following four actions.

1. Discover and practice being our *real self* or child within.
2. Identify our ongoing physical, mental-emotional and spiritual *needs*. Practice *getting* these needs *met* with safe and supportive people.
3. Identify, re-experience and *grieve* the pain of our *ungrieved*

losses or traumas in the presence of safe and supporting people.
4. Identify and work through our *core issues*.

These actions are closely related, although not listed in any particular order. Working on them, and thereby healing our true self or child within, generally occurs in a circular fashion, with work and discovery in one area a link to another area.

Vehicles, techniques or methods to assist us in this healing and recovery include:

Regular and Long Attendance at

1. *Self-help groups*, such as Co-Dependents Anonymous (CoDA), Al Anon, and Adult Children Anonymous, and
2. *Group therapy* that is specific for either co-dependence or adult children of dysfunctional families (this may take from three to five years of recovery work).[28,30]

As Needed

3. *"Detoxification"* from whatever person, place, thing, behavior or experience that may otherwise block the work of recovery from co-dependence.
4. Individual *counseling* or psychotherapy,
5. Inpatient or other *intensive* recovery experiences,
6. *Educational experiences* about co-dependence, and

An Ongoing Support System, which may include

7. Any of 1, 2, 3, or 4 above,
8. *Journaling*, or keeping a personal diary,
9. *Regular contact and sharing* with one or more trusted and safe friends, and
10. *Continuing, conscious contact* in a personal relationship with a Higher Power.

All of the above work more effectively if the person has first handled, through detoxification or detachment in some way, any active primary addictions or compulsions that may block ongoing recovery from co-dependence.

Recovery is neither easy nor short. For most, it takes from three to five years of a full recovery program, as described above. (I develop all of the above material in expanded form.)[28,29,30]

We have much to learn and to enjoy in our lives. Co-dependence can be our teacher.

REFERENCES

1. Adult Children of Alcoholics (ACA-Central Service Board) Box 35623, Los Angeles, CA 90028

2. Al-Anon Family Groups, P.O. Box 182, Madison Square Station, New York 10159

3. American Psychiatric Association DSM-III-R: Diagnostic and Statistical Manual of Mental Disorders (3rd ed.). Washington, DC, 1987

4. Anonymous: The Urantia (Earth) Book, Urantia Foundation, 533 Diversy Parkway, Chicago, IL 60614 (312-525-3319) 1955

5. Beattie M: Codependent No More. Hazelden, Center City, Minnesota, 1987

6. Bradshaw J: Bradshaw on the Family, PBS series, Houston, TX 1986

7. Cermak TL: Diagnosing & Treating Co-Dependence: A Guide for Professionals who Work with Chemical Dependents, Their Spouses, and Children. Johnson Institute, Minneapolis, MN, 1986

8. Co-Dependents Anonymous (CoDA), Box 5508, Glendale, AZ 85304 (602) 979-1751

9. A Course in Miracles. Foundation for Inner Peace. Tiburon, CA, 1976

10. DeRohan C: Right Use of Will: Healing & Evolving the Emotional Body. One World Publications, Santa Fe, NM 1986

11. Dossey L: Beyond Illness: Discovering the Experience of Health. Shambhala, Boulder, CO 1985

12. Guntrip H: Psychoanalytical Theory, Therapy and the Self: A Basic Guide to the Human Personality, in Freud, Erickson, Klein, Sullivan, Fairbairn, Hartman, Jacobsen and Winnicott. Basic Books, Harper Torchbooks, New York, 1973

13. Kellog T: Series of tapes on co-dependence & intimacy. 20300 Excelsior Boulevard, Minneapolis, MN 55331

14. Kohut H: The Analysis of the Self. International Universities Press, New York, 1971

15. Lazaris: Series of Spiritual-Psychological Teachings. Available from Concept Synergy, P.O. Box 159, Fairfax, CA 94930, (415) 456-4855

16. Matthews-Simonton S, in Simonton, Matthews-Simonton Cerighton: Getting Well Again. Bantam Books, New York, 1978

17. Mendenhall W: Course on co-dependence, Rutgers Summer School of Alcohol Studies, New Brunswick, NJ, June, 1987

18. Norwood R: Women Who Love Too Much. Tarcher, Los Angeles, CA, 1985

19. Pennebaker J et al.: SMU Study, Southern Methodist University, Dallas, TX, 1986

20. Rodegast P, Stanton J: Emmanuel's Book: A manual for living comfortably in the cosmos. Friend's Press, Box 1006, Weston, CT 06883, 1986

21. Schaef AW: Co-dependence: Misdiagnosed and Mistreated. Harper/Winston, Minneapolis, MN, 1986

22. Schaef AW: Personal communication, Baltimore, 1987

23. Subby R: Lost in the Shuffle: The Co-dependent Reality. Health Communications, Pompano Beach, FL, 1987

24. Siegel BS: Love, Medicine and Miracles: Lessons Learned About Self-Healing from a Surgeon's Experience with Exceptional Patients. Harper & Row, New York, 1986

25. Simos, BG: A Time to Grieve: Loss as a Universal Human Experience. Family Services Association of America, New York, 1979

26. Wapnick K: Christian Psychology in "A Course in Miracles." Foundation for Inner Peace. Box 635, Tiburon, CA 94920

27. Wegscheider-Cruse S: Choice-Making: For Co-Dependents, Adult Children and Spirituality Seekers. Health communications, Deerfield Beach, FL, 1985

28. Whitfield CL: Healing the Child Within: Discovery and Recovery for Adult Children of Dysfunctional Families. Health Communications, Deerfield Beach, FL, 1986

29. Whitfield CL: Alcoholism, Attachments, and Spirituality: Stress Management and Serenity During Recovery, A Transpersonal Approach. Tom Perrin, E. Rutherford, NJ (800) 321-7912, 1985

30. Whitfield CL: Wisdom to Know the Difference: Transforming Co-dependence into Healthy Relationships (working title of manuscript in process). 1989

31. Whitfield CL: Stress management & spirituality during recovery: a transpersonal approach. Three part article in Alcoholism Treatment Quarterly, Vol 1, No 1, 1984

Assessment of Co-dependency with Individuals from Alcoholic and Chemically Dependent Families

Ronald T. Potter-Efron, ACSW, PhD
Patricia S. Potter-Efron, BA, CAC

SUMMARY. A co-dependent is defined as someone who has been significantly affected in specific ways by current or past involvement in an alcoholic, chemically dependent or other long-term, highly stressful family environment. Specific effects include: (a) fear; (b) shame/guilt; (c) prolonged despair; (d) anger; (e) denial; (f) rigidity; (g) impaired identity development; and (h) confusion. These characteristics are detailed. A questionnaire is provided to assist the assessment process in each area. Additionally, implications for co-dependency treatment are noted.

DEFINITION OF CO-DEPENDENCY

Co-dependency is a term that is being used with increasing frequency in the field of chemical dependency treatment. Unfortunately, no clear definition of the term has emerged, which has led to confusion and loss of credibility. Frequently, the term has replaced the phrase "significant other" in AODA counseling and treatment and means very little except that the person has been exposed to another's alcohol or drug abuse or dependence. It is generally agreed that a co-dependent is someone whose life has been *significantly* affected by another person's use of alcohol or mood-altering chemicals. It is our belief that if co-dependency is to have value as a concept, it must be limited to those individuals who develop a series

Ronald T. Potter-Efron is affiliated with the Midelfort Clinic and Patricia S. Potter-Efron is in private practice, both in Eau Claire, WI.

37

of generally predictable and problematical responses from that exposure.

Several authors have attempted to clarify the concept of co-dependency. Sondra Smalley[1,2] defines co-dependency as a pattern of beliefs about life, learned behavior, and habitual feelings that make life painful. Her focus is on the external locus of control of the co-dependent person that makes the co-dependents rely on things outside of themselves for self-worth. Robert Subby[3] defines co-dependency as a dysfunctional pattern of living and problem solving which is nurtured by a set of rules within the family system. A more limited term, "Co-alcoholic," has been defined by Whitfield[4] as a pattern of ill health, maladaptive or problematic behavior that is associated with living, working with, or otherwise being close to an alcoholic. Greenleaf[5] distinguishes between "co-alcoholics," who are adults who help maintain the social and economic equilibrium of the alcoholic, and "para-alcoholics," children who grow up in a family with the alcohol syndrome and learn behavior from both the alcoholic and co-alcoholic parent. Cermak[6] suggests that co-dependency is one of a newly perceived class of problems that is simultaneously both interactive and intrapsychic in nature.

The effects of living in an alcoholic or similar family environment are so strong that an individual may be affected at any stage of life. Thus, children of alcoholics,[7] adult children of alcoholics[8,9] and adult spouses of alcoholics[10] all can suffer serious damage to their sense of reality, ability to trust, self-image, etc. Furthermore, this damage does not necessarily diminish when the immediate source of tension is removed. Co-dependents may continue to suffer serious consequences for years after their initial exposure, leading generally joyless, loveless and mindless[11] existences.

An important question is whether to limit this concept to families or to include individuals caught in other long-term highly stressful family environments. We consider the alcoholic family a model, a paradigm for which to gather information about co-dependency. Other family environments may produce a similar pattern, particularly those families with chronic hidden problems such as mental illness and incest. We believe that the term co-dependency should reflect this general pattern. The definition of co-dependency offered below reflects the need for a specific, limited concept that can be utilized in the assessment process:

A co-dependent is an individual who has been significantly affected in specific ways by current or past involvement in an alcoholic, chemically dependent, or other long-term, stressful family environment. Specific effects include: (a) fear; (b) shame/guilt; (c) prolonged despair; (d) anger; (e) denial; (f) rigidity; (g) impaired identity development; and (h) confusion.

ASSESSMENT OF CO-DEPENDENCY: OUTLINE OF MAJOR CHARACTERISTICS

Table I provides a list of the major characteristics most frequently found in co-dependent individuals. These characteristics will be discussed in detail in subsequent sections of this paper.

TABLE I

Co-dependency Assessment Criteria

A co-dependent is an individual who has been significantly affected in specific ways by current or past involvement in an alcoholic, chemically dependent, or other long-term, highly stressful family environment. Effects include: (a) fear; (b) shame/guilt; (c) prolonged despair; (d) anger; (e) denial; (f) rigidity; (g) impaired identity development; and (h) confusion.

Specifically, co-dependency can be assessed when:

1. The individual has been or is currently exposed to a long-term highly stressful family environment, including but not limited to alcohol dependency of another family member.

2. The individual reports (or is observed to have) at least 5 of the following 8 characteristics:

   a. Fear, indicated by:

      1. Preoccupation with problems of others
      2. Persistent anxiety and feelings of dread
      3. Avoidance of interpersonal risk, including low trust for others
      4. Controlling behavior — repeated and habitual

TABLE 1 (continued)

5. Over-responsibility
6. Manipulative attempts to alter the behavior of others, especially
   drinking behavior

b. Shame/Guilt, indicated by:

1. Persistent feelings of shame related both to own behavior and behavior of others
2. Persistent feelings of guilt about the problems of others
3. Isolation from others in order to hide family or personal shame
4. Self-hatred
5. Appearance of arrogance and superiority when linked with low self-
   worth

c. Prolonged Despair, indicated by:

1. Despair and hopelessness about changing current situation
2. Pessimistic world view
3. Low self-worth and sense of failure that does not reflect the individual's actual accomplishments

d. Anger, indicated by:

1. Persistent anger directed toward user, family, or self
2. Fear of loss of control if the individual becomes angry
3. Spiritual anger
4. Passive aggressive behavior, in particular toward the user

e. Denial, indicated by:

1. Consistent denial, particularly of source of family pain
2. Consistent minimization of severity of problem
3. Use of justifications that protect the user from negative consequences

f. Rigidity, indicated by:

1. Cognitive inflexibility
2. Behavioral inflexibility, including role rigidity
3. Moral/Spiritual inflexibility
4. Affective inflexibility — persistence of singular feeling states such as
   guilt, pity, anger

TABLE 1 (continued)

g. Impaired Identity Development, indicated by:

    1. Inability to make claims for self or take care of own needs
    2. Boundary separation difficulty—difficult to distinguish self from other, feeling other's pain
    3. Person dependency—needing other to validate self-worth, fear of being alone, obsessive concerns about how other perceives them

h. Confusion, indicated by:

    1. Persistent uncertainty about what is normal
    2. Persistent uncertainty about what is real
    3. Persistent uncertainty about feelings, including tendency to misidentify all feelings with one label
    4. Gullibility
    5. Indecisiveness

Pat and Ron Potter-Efron

CHARACTERISTICS OF CO-DEPENDENTS

Co-dependent families tend to undergo a set of processes that together produce particularly destructive consequences for their members. These processes develop as reactions to the presence of a continuing painful stimulus, the behavior of the alcoholic or similarly affected individual.

In the following discussion we will refer to alcoholic families. It should be understood that this limitation reflects primarily the utility of considering the alcoholic family as the paradigm for understanding co-dependent families. Much of what will be stated also applies to other highly stressed families.

Fear

"I know something bad will happen soon—it always does."

Residing in an alcoholic family often means living with fear and unpredictability. Uncertainty can become the norm, affecting every facet of daily life. For example, the whereabouts of the user may be unknown for long periods of time. Once the alcoholic does appear, there is the continuing uncertainty of how he or she will behave that day. Above all, there is the constant danger that something terrible could happen at any time to the alcoholic or family—an automobile accident, violent outburst, etc. Family members can become filled with a sense of dread about a future from which they can neither fight nor flee.

Additionally, the effects of alcoholism tend to permeate every sphere of daily life. For example, dinner times may become the setting for interminable harangues from an inebriated parent. Sexual encounters may be avoided by the spouse because they have become humiliating experiences. Isolation from previous friends may force the family to rely too much on each other. Furthermore, because of progressiveness, the user and family must pay increasingly more attention to problems created or enhanced by drinking behavior, whether the alcoholic is immediately present or not. The family tends to become preoccupied with the problem of how to manage the alcoholic so as to minimize their fear.

The cost of continually living in fear is high. Many co-dependents endure persistent feelings of anxiety and dread, coming to believe that anything good in their lives is in continuous and immediate danger of destruction. Co-dependents trust others poorly because in their experience their trust has been repeatedly betrayed by alcoholic erratic behavior.

Controlling behaviors emerge from this situation as desperate efforts to delay an inevitable disaster. The controller attempts repeatedly to protect the user from the consequences of his or her behavior, partly because those consequences—loss of life, job, place in the community—are feared to be too horrible to endure. The family members "hang on" to the alcoholic and become totally exhausted with the effort. Some family members become controllers in an attempt to regularize their environment. Responsibility shifts continually from the alcoholic toward the most caring and responsible members of the family: the chief enablers and family heroes. Meanwhile, lost children emotionally attempt to run away from the family but take their fear with them.

Manipulative behavior, such as watering down liquor supplies and lying to the alcoholic, is also a function of living in fear. Individuals violate their own value systems in an attempt to ensure the survival of the family. This distorted perspective must be confronted in therapy with care. The need of the co-dependent to maintain the safety of the entire family must be recognized.

Living in fear is indicated by six main personal characteristics: (1) preoccupation with the problems of others; (2) persistent anxiety; (3) avoidance of interpersonal risk; (4) controlling behavior; (5) over-responsibility; (6) manipulative behavior. Relevant questions in each of these areas include: (1) How much time do you spend worrying? About what? (2) How scary is it for you living in your home? When's the last time you felt safe? Do you expect angry outbursts or abuse? (3) Whom do you trust? (4) What have you done to try to control the user's drinking? (5) How responsible do you feel for the user? For the pain in your family? (6) Have you ever done anything sneaky to limit the user's drinking?

Shame/Guilt

"I deserve to be punished — I know I'm a bad person."

It is frequently a shaming experience to live with an alcoholic. Since alcoholism and chemical dependency are still considered moral weaknesses by large numbers of our society, living in an alcoholic family includes ongoing experiences of embarrassment and humiliation. Efforts at avoidance of public humiliation force the family away from potential sources of support so that they must rely increasingly upon each other. The family becomes isolated. Families in this situation frequently have a strongly stated rule that no one may ever talk about their problems to anyone outside the family.

The co-dependent individual is ashamed both about his own behavior and about the behavior of the alcoholic. Unable to distinguish clearly between self and other, the co-dependent is constantly vulnerable to disparaging comments about and from the user. The co-dependent is powerless to avoid shame-producing incidents since these behaviors originate outside of self.

As with the other characteristics mentioned above, this deep sense of shame goes on long enough that it may permanently affect the way family members perceive themselves in the world. They may come to believe they are much worse than others, that they are moral failures. They may see the family as the source of their shame and as family members believe that they will inevitably pass this moral weakness on to their offspring. Even when, as with some alcoholics, the co-dependent reacts against this inner shame by appearing arrogant, the underlying feelings of shame and worthlessness are likely to emerge during the therapeutic process.

Co-dependent individuals also may feel strong guilt, believing themselves responsible for the family pain. Although this guilt is irrational, in that the individual cannot be held responsible for the behavior of the alcoholic, nevertheless it may be deeply engrained. Guilt diverts the attention of co-dependent persons away from the alcoholic and towards themselves; co-dependents may spend tremendous amounts of energy in futile attempts to correct their shortcomings while failing to confront obvious problems with others in the family.

Five behaviors typically demonstrate a deep sense of shame or guilt in the co-dependent: (1) persistent feelings of shame about behavior of self and others; (2) persistent feelings of guilt about the problems of others; (3) isolation; (4) self-hatred; (5) arrogant behavior linked with low self-worth. Relevant questions for each area include: (1) When the user does something odd (dumb, crazy) how do you feel? (2) When something goes wrong in your family do you often feel guilty? (3) Do you find yourself avoiding anyone because of what happens in your family? Whom? (4) Are you a good or bad person? How do you know? What do you have to give others? (5) Do you sometimes act better than others when you really feel bad about yourself?

Prolonged Despair

"Things just keep getting worse and worse. Will this ever stop?"

A common characteristic of the co-dependent family experience is that it typically becomes steadily more severe over time. The exposed individual witnesses the continuing deterioration of the progressing alcoholic in a manner similar to the way that the spouse of an Alzheimer's disease victim must watch as the "soul" of the beloved husband or wife leaves the still functioning body.[12] As the basic personality of the alcoholic becomes submerged over time, the co-dependent learns that despair and hopelessness are a normal part of life. This is a learned helplessness because the family members slowly recognize that nothing they have done or given over years of time has kept the alcoholic from becoming relentlessly worse. This underlying sense of defeat may be masked, especially in those who play the role of family hero. Even these individuals will normally admit, however, when interviewed in depth, that they feel little sense of success and are certain that they are intrinsically inadequate and valueless.

Three subcategories have been listed for prolonged despair: (1) despair and hopelessness about changing the current situation; (2) pessimistic world view; (3) low self-worth and a sense of failure that does not reflect the individual's actual accomplishments. Useful questions that may be asked of the interviewee for each of these areas include: (1) How sad do you feel about what has happened in your family? Do you ever feel you don't care what happens? Do you feel like giving up? (2) How much hope do you have that life will get better? Do you think of yourself as an optimist or pessimist — and has that changed lately? (3) Do you think of yourself as a failure? Why? When somebody praises you, how do you respond?

It is highly recommended that individuals who appear strongly involved in prolonged despair be monitored carefully for clinical depression. Suicidal ideation may be present and must be investigated.

Anger

"I feel cheated by my husband. He's ruined my life."

Co-dependent individuals often believe they have been cheated. Trapped in a painful environment, many become chronically angry at the alcoholic, their family, the world, God, and themselves. This anger may be directly expressed at the alcoholic or it may be deflected onto others, creating a family scapegoat who distracts the family from its real issues. The co-dependent may become a "nagging bitch," lashing out at the alcoholic and ultimately getting blamed for causing his drinking. With great frequency, the co-dependent blames himself or herself for continuing to live in this miserable condition, adding self-hatred to his or her repertoire of self-defeating feelings, thoughts, and behaviors.

The co-dependent may become more than merely angry when the feeling is of great strength and duration. In this situation a better term is rage, sometimes expressed in explosive episodes and sometimes experienced as a slow but engulfing feeling that never goes away. If stifled, the rage leads toward depression and occasionally suicide. If unresolved, it may come out in the form of confusing over-reactions to ordinary minor frustrations or in physical problems such as ulcers, hypertension, or arthritic syndromes.

The co-dependent individual may fear complete loss of control if he ever admits or gives in to his anger. Thus, the co-dependent does not feel free to explore the expression of anger at a less than explosive level. One result may be that, unable to direct this anger at its proper source, the co-dependent may become passively aggressive, quietly but efficiently sabotaging the alcoholic and anyone who might offer help.

A co-dependent may feel betrayed by God and have a long-term spiritual crisis. It is important to ask specifically about this form of anger, since many co-dependent individuals might feel to ashamed or guilty to volunteer this information. The acknowledgement of spiritual anger in religious clients during the assessment phase of treatment may itself help begin a reconciliation process in this sphere.

Anger is best noted by evidence of: (1) persistent anger; (2) fear of loss of control; (3) spiritual anger; (4) passive aggressive behavior. Relevant questions in each area include: (1) How mad are you about what has happened to you (your family)? (2) What would happen if you ever got really mad? (3) Are you angry at God? Is it all right to be angry at God? (4) Are there any little ways you get back at the user? How? In what three ways can you upset the user any time?

Denial

"How could I live with her all these years and not notice her problem?"

Denial and minimization, characteristic of both alcoholics and their families, is a cognitive process that serves to lessen feelings of fear and shame. Even as alcoholic behavior increasingly pervades the life of the user and family, some or all of these individuals may refuse to recognize or act upon this evidence. The denial allows abnormal behavior to be treated as normal and contributes to increasing the severity of the problem.

Justifications, such as blaming friends of the user for his problem or making excuses to employers, serve the same purpose. Additionally, they deflect consequences of irresponsible alcoholic behavior away from the alcoholic and toward more safe targets. The co-dependent will often accept blame himself for these behaviors, contributing to his low self-worth.

The denial process can be noted when the following characteristics are observed or reported: (1) consistent denial, in particular of alcohol related problems; (2) minimization of the seriousness of the problem; (3) repeated justifications for the irresponsible behavior of the alcoholic.

Relevant questions in each area include: (1) How have you tried not to see what is going on in your family? Why are you here now? What thoughts or feelings have you tried to avoid? (2) How have you tried to minimize the seriousness of the problem? (3) What excuses have you made to justify the user's behavior?

Rigidity

"Everything seems black and white now."

Flexibility in feelings, thoughts and behavior is a relative luxury in personal development, easily disrupted or broken down during periods of stress. Co-dependents, absorbed in the problems of another and confused about their own identities, tend to grasp at whatever structures they can find that appear to give meaning to their situation. Clinging tenaciously to these interpretations of reality, they may become unable to change important aspects of their lives.

Co-dependents demonstrate several types of rigidity. Cognitively, they tend to think in "either/or," "black and white" patterns. Behaviorally, they may develop inflexible daily routines. Spiritually and morally, "good/bad" decisions are made based on absolute standards of expected behavior. Emotionally, the co-dependent tends to become locked into singular feeling states, such as guilt, anger, or pity. Role rigidity of the family of the alcoholic is common.

Rigidity can be observed through evidence of: (1) cognitive inflexibility; (2) behavioral inflexibility, including role rigidity; (3) spiritual/moral inflexibility; (4) affective inflexibility. Relevant questions for each area include: (1) How hard is it for you to think of new solutions for your problems? Do you often think in black and white terms? (2) Do you get stuck in unbreakable routines? How flexible is your household in splitting up jobs? (3) Can you be both a good and bad person? Do you think of the user as a bad or sinful person? (4) How many feelings have you had lately? Do you seem always to be made, sad, etc.? What feelings do you avoid?

Impaired Identity Development

"I don't even know who I am!"

Preoccupied and afraid, the co-dependent individual has become fixated upon alcohol and the alcoholic behavior of the user. Not able to take time for self, the co-dependent may come to believe that he has no right to express personal wants or needs. The cost to family members in this situation is that they have little energy left to direct to their own developmental needs. They may fail to mature emotionally and spiritually. They slowly lose or never gain the ability to answer the question "Who am I?" and find themselves feeling incomplete. The boundary between themselves and others may be so permeable that they cannot tell where they end and others begin. Having spent so much time focused on alcohol and so little time on themselves, family members often function as partial persons—dependent upon others to make their lives meaningful, exciting, and whole. They become "person dependent." The continuing need to complete one's self through external validation compels codependents into movement away from the self. Unable to take the time to appreciate themselves, they remain emotionally and spiritually empty.

Impaired identity development can be documented through evidence of: (1) inability to care for self; (2) boundary separation difficulty; (3) person dependency. Relevant questions for each area include: (1) When is the last time you did something good for yourself? What? Do you feel selfish when you take care of yourself? (2) Do you believe you can feel other people's pain? The user's pain? Do you ever feel empty, as if part of you is missing? Who are you? (3) How much do you worry about what people think of you? When do you know you are a good person?

Confusion

"I don't know what being normal is."

The alcoholic family experience can be so confusing that many co-dependents are left with permanent uncertainties about what is real. In part, this confusion is a result of a need to hide from fear and shame. Although the effects of alcohol become pervasive in many families, there are unspoken rules that prevent open communication about the problem. Faced with these rules, the co-dependent learns to doubt the reality before his or her eyes. This "crazy-making" behavior is similar to that reported by R. D. Laing with schizophrenic families.[13] In both situations, the concerned family member receives "you are crazy" messages when he or she correctly perceives the situation, and "you are not crazy" messages when he or she joins in a collective denial system.

Confusion of this magnitude, repeated over months and years, leaves the co-dependent cognitively damaged. As Woititz[14] notes, one of the strongest characteristics of the adult children of alcoholics is that they do not know what is normal. Doubting their own perceptions, they must rely on others to tell them about normalcy, making them repeatedly gullible to cognitive manipulation. This gullibility is one of the more striking aspects of co-dependency. Again and again, the co-dependent allows himself to be manipulated with arguments patently absurd to neutral observers. The co-dependent accepts these arguments, because the co-dependent has no faith in his or her own cognitive ability to assess reality.

Another aspect of confusion is uncertainty about feelings. Co-dependent individuals have trouble correctly identifying their feelings because some or all feelings have been disallowed and denied in their families. As a result co-dependents tend either to doubt all their feelings or to identify all affect by one acceptable label. For example, an individual may think he is angry when in fact he is feeling love toward another.

Even though the co-dependent does not trust others he learns to trust himself even less. This uncertainty produces cognitive and behavior indecisiveness. If pressed the co-dependent may desperately make impulsive decisions to relieve tension but these decisions may well be negated the next day.

Confusion is demonstrated by: (1) uncertainty about reality; (2) uncertainty about normalcy; (3) uncertainty about feelings, including misidentification of all feeling with one label; (4) gullibility; (5) indecisiveness. Relevant questions in each area include: (1) Does anyone in your family tell you that you are crazy to think or feel the way you do? Do you wonder if what you think you see is real? How confused are you? (2) Is your situation normal? How do you know? (3) Do you know what you are feeling? How do you know when you are mad, sad, etc.? (4) What excuses does the user give you? How gullible are you? Do you get taken advantage of a lot? (5) How hard is it for you to make up your mind?

CO-DEPENDENCY ASSESSMENT QUESTIONNAIRE

Table II is a closed question format assessment instrument designed to elicit information about co-dependency directly from the client. Each question is a probe of the parallel assessment criterion listed in Table I. Thus, question "1a" refers to criterion "1a" in Table I.

As noted in Table II, it is necessary to score two positive answers in each major segment for that area to be considered positive for co-dependency. For example, if a client answers yes to only question "1a," that individual would not be considered to have demonstrated the general characteristic of fear. Similarly, an individual must be scored positive in at least five of the eight general categories to be labelled co-dependent. These criteria have been adopted in order to provide consistent and relatively conservative guidelines for co-dependency assessment and treatment.

The authors have found that it is necessary to specify a time frame when utilizing the above questionnaire. For example, asking the respondent to indicate which questions they would have an-

TABLE II

Co-dependency Assessment

Name _____   Date _____

A co-dependent is an individual who has been significantly affected in specific ways by current or past involvement in an alcoholic, chemically dependent, or other long-term highly stressful family environment. Long-term illness, physical or psychiatric, can be a basis for this stress, as well as drug abuse of prescribed or unprescribed medications.

Specifically, co-dependency can be assessed when:

_____ The person has been exposed to a long-term highly stressful environment. Note the nature and duration of this situation below:

_____

_____

_____

AND

_____ The individual reports (or is observed to have) at least five of the following eight characteristics which are grouped below. At least two questions must be answered "yes" in any major area for that area to be considered positive for co-dependency.

	Yes	No
1. Fear:		
a. Do you become preoccupied with the problems of others, especially those of the user?	_____	_____
b. Do you try to "keep things under control" or "keep a handle" on situations?	_____	_____
c. Do you take more than your fair share of responsibility for tasks that have to be done?	_____	_____
d. Are you afraid to approach others directly, in particular the user?	_____	_____
e. Do you often have anxious feelings or worry about what will happen next?	_____	_____
f. Do you avoid taking risks with others because it is hard for you to trust?	_____	_____

TABLE II (continued)

	Yes	No

2. <u>Shame/Guilt:</u>

   a. Do you often feel ashamed not only about your behavior, but also about the behavior of others, especially the user?
   b. Do you feel guilty about the problems of others in
   your family?
   c. Do you withdraw from social contact when you are
   feeling upset?
   d. Do you sometimes hate yourself?
   e. Do you ever cover up bad feelings about yourself by
   acting too confidently?

3. <u>Prolonged Despair:</u>

   a. Do you often feel hopeless about changing the current situation?
   b. Do you tend to be pessimistic about the world in
   general?
   c. Do you have a sense of low self-worth or failure that
   does not reflect your skills and accomplishments?

4. <u>Rage:</u>

   a. Do you feel persistently angry with the user, other
   family members, or yourself?
   b. Are you afraid of losing control if you let yourself
   get really mad?
   c. Are you angry at God?
   d. Do you ever get back at others in sneaky ways, perhaps without being fully aware of this behavior at
   the time?

5. <u>Denial:</u>

   a. Do you feel yourself denying the basic problems in
   your family?
   b. Do you tell yourself that these problems are not *that*
   bad?
   c. Do you find reasons to justify the irresponsible behavior of others in your family?

6. <u>Rigidity:</u>

   a. Do you tend to think in either/or terms when there
   are problems, instead of looking at many alternatives?

TABLE II (continued)

	Yes	No
b. Do you feel troubled if anyone upsets your usual routines?		
c. Do you tend to see moral issues in black-and-white terms?		
d. Do you "get stuck" in certain feelings such as guilt, love or anger?		

7. <u>Impaired Identity Development:</u>

	Yes	No
a. Do you have trouble asking for what you want and need?		
b. Do you feel pain right along with another person who is in pain?		
c. Do you need to have another person around in order for you to feel worthwhile?		
d. Do you worry a great amount about how others perceive you?		

8. <u>Confusion:</u>

	Yes	No
a. Do you wonder what it means to be "normal"?		
b. Do you sometimes think that you must be "crazy"?		
c. Do you find it difficult at times to identify what you are feeling?		
d. Do you have a tendency to be taken in by others – to be gullible?		
e. Do you have a hard time making up your mind – are you indecisive?		

Other Observations of the Interviewer:

Recommendations:

Signature _____   Date _____

Developed by Pat and Ron Potter-Efron, Rt. 4, Box 229, Eau Claire, WI 54701. Please notify Pat and Ron if you adapt this format for assessment of co-dependency. Thank you.

swered positively at the time they were most troubled by another person's use of alcohol or drugs will produce the highest co-dependency ratings. Contrasting those answers with the current functioning of the client may help document how that individual has grown or changed over time.

THE ASSESSMENT PROCESS
AND TREATMENT IMPLICATIONS

One problem with attempting to assess co-dependency is that each individual is only a part of a complex interactional process. The family as a whole must be assessed, if possible, for the central characteristics mentioned above. Nevertheless, it is often necessary to diagnose and treat a single individual outside of his or her family context. The following guidelines are offered for this individual effort.

1. Clearly focus the assessment interview upon the behavior, thoughts and feelings of the possible co-dependent. Utilizing phrases such as "How has all this behavior of your spouse (child, parents) affected you?" "Right now I'm interested in you," and "Before we can help him (her) I need to find out more about you" will speed up the assessment while helping the co-dependent begin the difficult transition from looking at the behavior of others to looking at self.

2. In addition to determining the existence of co-dependent characteristics, it is also important to gauge the severity of personal impairment in each area. For example, a particular individual may demonstrate relatively more severe problems with confusion than shame. The initial focus can then be molded appropriately.

3. Similarly, it is important to notice the general severity of co-dependent impairment. This can be measured by how completely the co-dependent pattern of living compels individual behavior. At one extreme are those persons whose lives are almost completely ruled by their co-dependency. At this level, co-dependency is both chronic and severe. Intensive therapy may be needed. People with this chronic pattern will probably need a daily Al Anon program both during and after counseling. These individuals display very

erratic progress in treatment in that they tend to return to denial repeatedly.

Less strongly affected co-dependents are more amenable to less intensive therapy. These persons tend to lead relatively normal lives in many areas, only displaying co-dependent patterns when faced with strong stressors and appropriate family cues. For example, they may report that they are independent at work, but that they become different persons in the presence of a demanding alcoholic. They are more likely to respond quickly to standard individual and group therapy. Weekly Al Anon meetings are highly recommended.

Finally, there is a group of co-dependents who have been damaged only slightly. Often, these are spouses of alcoholics who did not grow up in alcoholic families and whose husband or wife has only recently developed an alcoholic lifestyle. These individuals are candidates primarily for education or brief individual and family programs. They are capable, with minimal help, of breaking from the co-dependency pattern and returning to a previously more satisfying way of life.

4. It is possible that some individuals might exhibit apparent co-dependent behaviors only in non-family situations. The work setting, in particular, is often cited because of its stressful nature. Individuals exhibiting these limited indicators should be carefully checked for the presence of a hidden highly stressful family background. If no indications are found we recommend these individuals not be diagnosed as co-dependents. Rather, they should be further assessed for possible depression, adjustment disorders, or personality disorders.

5. Grandchildren of alcoholics may become co-dependent. The operating factor here is the inappropriate co-dependent behavior of the untreated middle generation parent.

6. Many alcoholics are also co-dependent. Initial treatment for these persons should focus on their alcoholism. However, it must be recognized that untreated co-dependency issues contribute to alcoholic relapse. We recommend that counselors in treatment programs complete an assessment for co-dependency as a standard component of their intake process. Co-dependency treatment as a

complement for primary alcohol treatment can then be initiated as needed during treatment and in continuing care.

CONCLUSION

A co-dependent has been defined in this article as someone who has been significantly affected in specific ways by current or past involvement in an alcoholic, chemically dependent, or other long-term, highly stressful family environment. Specific effects include: (a) fear; (b) shame/guilt; (c) prolonged despair; (d) anger; (e) denial; (f) rigidity; (g) impaired identity development; and (h) confusion. Each of these effects has been detailed in the text. A questionnaire has been provided to help the assessor determine the extent to which the co-dependency process has impaired the normal development and functioning of each individual. Finally, implications for co-dependency treatment are noted.

REFERENCES

1. Smalley, Sondra, "Co-Dependency: An Intimacy Dilemma," 1982 SBS Publications, 185 Windsor Court, New Brighton, MN 55112.
2. Smalley, Sondra, "Co-Dependency: An Introduction," 1982 SBS Publications, 185 Windsor Court, New Brighton, MN 55112.
3. Subby, Robert and John Forel, "Co-Dependency and Family Rules," 1983 Health Communications, Inc., Hollywood, FL.
4. Whitfield, Charles, "Co-Dependency: An Emerging Illness Among Professionals," Focus on Alcohol and Drug Issues, Vol. 6, No. 3, May 1983.
5. Greenleaf, J. "Co-Alcoholic/Paraalcoholic," Paper presented at the National Council on Alcoholism National Forum, New Orleans, 1981.
6. Cermak, Timmen, "Children of Alcoholics and the Case for New Diagnostic Category of Codependency," Alcohol Health and Research World, Summer, 1984, pp. 38-41.
7. Ackerman, Robert, Children of Alcoholics, 2nd ed., 1983, Learning Publications, Inc., P. O. Box 1325 Holmes Beach, FL 33509.
8. Black, Claudia. It Will Never Happen to Me. M. A. G. Printing, Denver, CO, 1982.
9. Woititz, Janet, Adult Children of Alcoholics. Health Communications, Hollywood, FL, 1983.
10. Wegscheider, Sharon, Another Chance: Hope and Health for the Alcoholic Family, 1982, Science and Behavior Books, Palo Alto, CA.

11. Steiner, Claude, *Scripts People Live*, 1974, Random House, New York.
12. Kapust, Lissa, "Living with Dementia: The Ongoing Funeral," Social Work in Health Care, vol 7 (7) Summer 1982, pp. 79-91.
13. Laing, R. D., *Sanity, Madness, and the Family*, New York, Basic Books, 1971.
14. Woititz, op. cit.

System Dynamics in Alcoholic Families

Mary Talley Erekson, MA
Steven E. Perkins, PhD

The impact of alcohol abuse on family functioning, so obvious to clinicians, has sparked a growing interest in a systemic perspective on alcoholism. Traditionally, many of the articles dealing with the effects of alcoholism have taken the individual-oriented approach, viewing the non-drinkers in the family as passive victims. However, a few have begun to advocate the adoption of a systemic perspective on alcoholics and their families, which views all members as active participants in the creation of a family problem (Steinglass, 1982; Wilson, 1982; Jacob and Seilhamer, 1982).

The systems approach focuses on the patterns of interaction that characterize current family relationships, rather than focusing on individual members. The model assumes that the family as a system has properties that cannot be identified with any one member (Minuchin, 1974; Umana, Gross, and McConville, 1981). The properties usually concern family processes, or the way family members do things, as opposed to family content, or what they say to each other.

Two clusters of family systems concepts appear to be useful in describing the behavior seen in alcoholics and their families. The first is the notion of *patterned behavior*. Jackson (1967) states that an individual relates to another through patterned behavior or redundancies, which can be described as rules for governing family interaction. The concept of roles also fits this cluster of patterned

---

Mary Talley Erekson is Family Therapist at the Akron Family Institute, Akron, OH. Steven E. Perkins is Founder and Director of the Akron Family Institute, Akron, OH and Adjunct Associate Professor of Education, University of Akron, Akron, OH.

behavior, since roles refer to regularly performed behaviors and are usually maintained by implicit rules. In this paper, the terms patterns, rules, roles and redundancies will refer to the idea of regularly recurring interactions.

The second cluster of family systems concepts that may be useful for understanding alcoholics and their families concerns the notion of *family structure*. Minuchin (1974) suggests that the family develops a structure as it differentiates and carries out its functions through subsystems. Individuals or any combination of members within the family are called subsystems. For instance, a husband and wife form a special type of subsystem when they guide and direct the affairs of their children. They operate as a parental subsystem. The structure or organization in this family would be very different from that of a family which has a subsystem of mother and oldest daughter directing the children's activities. Boundaries are an important part of subsystems, since the boundaries of a subsystem are basically the rules defining who participates and how. In the previous example, if the wife says to her husband, "You don't need to talk to Johnny about playing with your tools. Mary will take care of it," the parental subsystem is being defined as mom and oldest child.

For proper family functioning the boundaries of subsystems must be clear. They must be defined well enough to allow subsystems' members to carry out their functions without interference and at the same time allow contact between members of the subsystem and others. Minuchin (1974) states that the composition of a subsystem is not nearly as significant as the clarity of its boundaries and that the clarity of subsystem boundaries within a family is a useful parameter for evaluating family functioning. Families tend to fall somewhere along a continuum ranging from overly rigid boundaries to clear but flexible boundaries, to unclear, diffuse boundaries. In families with overly rigid boundaries, communication across subsystems is difficult, restricted and often ignored, and the protective functions of the family are handicapped. Members of the subsystems are distant from one another, both communicatively and emotionally. In families with unclear, diffuse boundaries, there is an increase in communication, concern and sensitivity among family members to the extent that boundaries become blurred. With these family members, individuality is underemphasized and identities blend. These two extremes of boundary functioning are called disengagement and enmeshment (Minuchin, 1974).

It is common in the alcoholism literature to see reports of how an alcoholic has affected his/her spouse and/or children. The concept of subsystems in families, however, suggests that the effect an alcoholic has in the family may itself be affected by all other subsystems. Wilson (1982) suggests, in fact, that the impact of alcoholism on children is related to family dysfunction and that family dysfunction may be both a cause and an effect of alcoholic behavior. For instance, the alcoholism of one spouse has an effect on the other spouse, often before children ever appear on the scene. How the non-alcoholic spouse responds to the alcoholic and how the alcoholic in turn responds to his/her spouse sets the stage for certain redundancies or patterns to occur. Consequently, as children join the family system, they are not simply affected by the drinking spouse, but also by the patterns and redundancies the marital dyad has developed up to that point. This suggests that the responses of the non-drinking spouse may play a large role in the effect of alcohol abuse on children and also on the drinking spouse. The addition of children, or the sibling subsystem, has an effect on the marital dyad and creates a new parental subsystem. Patterns or redundancies begin to shift as the spousal unit adapts to parental duties. Whatever parental patterns appear impact the sibling subsystem, and the children's responses to parental functions in turn affect the parental subsystem. By the same token, the impact of the siblings on the parental subsystems has implications for the spousal subsystem and, because that spousal subsystem is intertwined with alcohol, alcohol use will somehow be affected. A diagram of how these subsystems are linked and affect each other is shown in Figure 1 with the arrows indicating an interactional effect. Consequently, alcohol use reverberates through the family system, but its impact may be mediated by the repetitive patterns developed within the subsystem.

The remainder of this paper will offer research findings and clinical observations of the effects of alcoholism on the family with the intent of describing interactional patterns. These patterns will be

FIGURE 1.

THE RELATIONSHIP OF ALCOHOL USE TO FAMILY SUBSYSTEMS

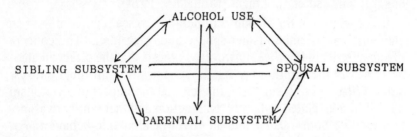

described within the context of each subsystem, integrating the subsystems to show the mediating effects.

ALCOHOL – A SPECIAL PROBLEM
FOR SYSTEMS PERSPECTIVE

The ability to make concise, generalized statements about family interactions is complicated and hampered by two special properties of alcoholism. The first is that alcoholism by definition involves progressively greater use of alcohol, or at least greater deterioration in personal functioning with sustained use. Consequently, family interactions will change in some way just because the alcoholic's condition becomes worse. The literature is scattered with research dealing with the developmental effect of alcohol on family functioning (Downs, 1982; Jackson, 1954; James and Goldman, 1971; Lemert, 1960), and clinicians see obvious differences in families where alcoholism is in the early stages, as opposed to when it is a well-established part of the family functioning. When looking at the family system, then, it is important to realize that interaction patterns will change and shift, even if only in intensity, frequency and/ or duration of behaviors. The discussion of family interaction patterns here will suffer from the fact that research which reports family behavior is frequently not categorized in any way according to the degree of dependency exhibited by the alcoholic spouse.

A second special property of alcoholism also affects our ability to make specific statements about family patterns and functioning. Alcoholism is characterized by periods of sobriety and periods of intoxication. It does not take research to establish that an intoxicated person behaves differently than a sober one and consequently affects family interaction patterns differently at different times. This difference, like the developmental aspect of alcoholism, is a variable which needs more attention in order to clearly define family interactional patterns.

ALCOHOLISM AND THE SPOUSAL SUBSYSTEM

Even given the problems discussed above, there are trends in the literature concerning interactional patterns in spousal subsystems where one spouse is an alcoholic. A considerable body of information suggests that the marital relation is characterized by critical, hostile, and disapproving communication (Jacob, Ritchey, Cvitkovic, and Blane, 1981). Investigations into the coping styles of non-alcoholic spouses show increasing hostility between partners as alcoholism progresses (Gorad, 1971; Jacob et al., 1981; James and Goldman, 1971; Orford and Guthrie, 1976) and an increase in negative affect in the presence of alcohol (Jacob et al., 1981). The alcoholic and his/her spouse appear to respond to each other with increasing hostility over time in general and specifically during periods of intoxication, suggesting a growing cycle of hostility and resentment. While this pattern receives the most support from formal research, there are indications that other coping styles may characterize a non-alcoholic's response to the alcoholic. In addition to hostility, Orford and Guthrie (1976) have identified four more coping styles for non-alcoholic spouses: protecting the alcoholic, withdrawing within the marriage (by avoiding the spouse and avoiding feelings), safeguarding family interests (by keeping children out of the way and hiding valuables from the spouse), and acting out (by trying to provoke the alcoholic through getting drunk himself/herself or trying to make him/her jealous). Although the experimental evidence is not strong for these additional styles, clinical observations seems to support them, at least roughly. Clinically, non-alcoholic spouses are frequently seen engaged in behaviors that protect the alcoholic, that isolate himself/herself from the alcoholic or that manipulate the alcoholic.

From a systemic perspective, however, the interesting aspect of these coping behaviors is that they serve to support the alcoholism by shielding the alcoholic in one way or another from the natural consequences of his/her use (Mendenhall, 1986), or by giving him/her cause to rationalize the drinking. Then, as alcoholism progresses, greater coping is required. James and Goldman (1971) found that progressive drinking and greater use of all of the above coping styles do accompany each other. Not only is alcohol use an important part of this subsystem's functioning, but the spouse's coping style is as well, and each of these redundancies affects the other.

Another group of studies focuses on the periodic nature of alcoholism. Steinglass (1982) found that interaction patterns for couples were different when the partner was drinking than when that partner was abstinent. It was not just the alcoholic's behavior that changed, but also the spouse's, indicating a sobriety-intoxication pattern for both spouses. Rather than finding specific patterns used by each couple, they found a more complex set of patterns. A couple's intoxicated pattern was often the opposite of their sobriety interaction. For instance, a couple who showed distance between them while the husband was sober became closer when the husband was intoxicated. They also found that during intoxication both spouses' behavior was more highly patterned. There was less flexibility and variety in their interaction. A third interesting finding was that both spouses were unable to accurately assess their intoxicated pattern. Some researchers have suggested that this on-off cycling, or change from intoxicated to sober interactional patterns poses a special problem to the non-alcoholic spouse, who has to live with constant inconsistency (Downs, 1982; Steinglass, 1982). The non-alcoholic spouse has constantly-changing roles and is adapting and readapting to first an intoxicated spouse, then a sober one. For instance, studies have indicated that wives take over more problem-solving functions while husbands are intoxicated (Jacob et al., 1981), but this pattern shifts while the husband is sober and the wife has to relinquish some of these functions. Downs (1981) suggests that this shifting in patterns becomes more marked as alcoholism progresses and signals the beginning of a secondary crisis. Eventually the non-alcoholic spouse may be confronted with enough environmental chaos to succumb to a loss of daily structure (Mendenhall, 1986).

The result of the repeated interactions is that one spouse develops alcoholism and the other spouse develops a co-dependency problem. Co-dependency is defined as a primary condition resulting from stress produced by living in a committed relationship with an alcoholic person (Mendenhall, 1986). In other words, the non-alcoholic spouse develops a regular set of reactive behaviors to the alcoholic, and these behaviors may increase in frequency and intensity. Unfortunately, reactive behaviors usually serve to increase drinking rather than to decrease it. As the drinking increases, the reactive behavior of the spouse – while usually intended to decrease drinking – actually helps to keep it going, and a vicious cycle is in effect.

As mentioned earlier, one way to assess the level of family dysfunction is to examine the clarity of the boundaries around the subsystem (Minuchin, 1974). In the spousal subsystem the boundary which needs to be clear is the boundary between husband and wife. This boundary needs to be diffuse enough to allow communication flow between them, but rigid enough to differentiate the husband and wife from each other. Boundaries are a problem in alcoholic spousal subsystems in two ways. First, because of the sober-intoxicated pattern suggested by Steinglass (1982) it would seem that the boundary between husband and wife would be in flux and consequently not too clear, contributing to confusion in the spousal subsystem. In addition to initial boundary shifts, a second problem from clinical observation is that the boundary between husband and wife eventually becomes too diffuse or too rigid. For instance, when the boundary is too diffuse and the level of engagement or enmeshment between spouses is too great, the clinician sees a non-using spouse who may argue, hit, please, or get drunk himself/herself in an attempt to decrease the spouse's drinking. In this instance the non-alcoholic spouse does not sufficiently differentiate himself/herself from the alcoholic. Somehow the alcoholic's problem has become the non-alcoholic's problem to fix. In addition, because of the diffuse boundary, any individual problem one of the spouses encounters is amplified to the other spouse. The alcoholic may respond to amplified problems by drinking more, and the co-dependent spouse by trying even harder with the previous methods, which do not work. The stage is set for escalation of both their problems.

Clinical observations indicate that the boundary between husband and wife can also become too rigid, where communication is restricted and the spouses are unable to perform protective functions for each other. When the spouses avoid each other or refuse to talk to each other, they become disengaged and it takes an increasingly extreme situation by one spouse to get a message across the rigid boundary and evoke a response from the other spouse. Consequently, if the alcoholic has a big enough crisis, the spouse might respond in some way, and if the spouse provokes an extreme crisis, the alcoholic might respond in some way. It is easy to see how conflict could escalate as each spouse comes to rely on providing crises to establish contact with each other. The result of this too-rigid boundary, interestingly enough, is the same as the result of the too-diffuse boundary: the alcoholic drinks more, while the co-dependent spouse becomes more extreme and habitual in his/her unproductive pattern.

Orford et al. (1975) suggest that "the dimension of engagement-disengagement may be crucial in indicating the state of a family system complicated by excessive drinking in the husband, and may give an indication of the potential for immediate change" (p. 1265). From this standpoint it is clear that alcohol is now not the only problem the spousal subsystem faces. They have developed dysfunctional ways of family relating.

THE EFFECT OF THE SPOUSAL SUBSYSTEM ON THE PARENTAL SUBSYSTEM

When children enter the family, the creation of the parental subsystem will reflect, in some way, the issues, problems, and concerns that the alcoholic spousal couple is grappling with. Earlier it was discussed that in an alcoholic/non-alcoholic spouse relationship there is likely to be a cycle of hostility and resentment, and that the non-alcoholic spouse may get stuck in patterns of protecting the alcoholic, safeguarding the family, acting out in an effort to control the alcoholic, or manipulating the alcoholic, in an attempt to decrease his drinking. It was noted that the fluctuation between sobriety and intoxication patterns kept roles and functions of the spouses in a state of flux, and that the clarity, diffuseness and rigidity of the spousal subsystem boundaries often led to supporting the alcoholism and increasing family dysfunction. The addition of the parental subsystem creates a new arena for old problems. The greater differentiation of the system (now consisting of a spousal subsystem and a parental subsystem) makes a higher level of complexity possible, and the potential for dysfunction to escalate becomes greater.

The literature on the effect of the spousal subsystem on the parental subsystem in the families of alcoholics is sparse, but some speculations can be made based upon the literature on parenting problems in alcoholic families. First, it seems logical that angry, resentful spouses are going to be in some measure angry, resentful parents. The literature does indicate that spousal anger is transferred to parental anger. Co-dependent spouses and alcoholic spouses both engage in scapegoating (Mendenhall, 1986), and clinical observations frequently record at least one scapegoated child in alcoholic families (Wegscheider, 1981). There are also indications that co-dependent spouses' habitual reactions to the alcoholism result in a loss of daily structure (Mendenhall, 1986; Morehouse and Richards, 1983; Jacob, Favorini, Meisel, and Anderson, 1978), indecision (Mendenhall, 1986), inability to set and stick to limits with children, emotional neglect of children (Morehouse and Richards, 1983; Cork, 1969) or overinvolvement with children (Mendenhall, 1986). Each of these parental problems may be related to interactions developed in the spousal subsystem. For instance: (1) the co-dependent spouse who withdraws within the marriage and becomes isolated and the spousal subsystem characterized by rigid boundaries and restricted communication might well produce emotionally neglected children; (2) the co-dependent spouse who protects the family and the spousal subsystem characterized by diffuse boundaries and heightened concern might show overinvolvement with children; (3) the confusion and role changes produced by the fluctuating sobriety and intoxication patterns may result in the loss of daily structure and indecision concerning parental limits for children. While these examples are simplistic, some of the basic threads woven into the spousal subsystem seem to appear in the fabric of the parental subsystem. In addition, it is not drinking alone, but the mediating effects of the subsequent interactional patterns that help determine family functioning. Additional support for this idea comes from the fact that children report that quarreling and fighting is more of a concern to them than drinking (Booz, Allen, and Hamilton, Inc., 1974; Wilson, 1982).

In addition to interactional patterns which show up as threads woven through the spousal and parental subsystems, the nature of the boundaries between the spousal and parental subsystem will mediate the effect of alcoholism in the family. The boundary between the spousal subsystem and the parental subsystem needs to be diffuse enough to allow the marriage partners to communicate both as spouses and as parents, but rigid enough to differentiate the spousal and parental functions. Downs (1982) has suggested that the boundaries between spousal and parental subsystems in alcoholic families become more fluid when the alcoholic alternates between being a spouse and a child who needs to be taken care of. As that spouse becomes less able to fulfill spousal roles or parental roles, a child might periodically enter either subsystem to take over for the alcoholic spouse. An example of this structural confusion would be an alcoholic father who acts like a brother to his son, or a son who acts as a parent to the rest of the siblings. On top of this, the structure may shift according to whether the alcoholic is sober or intoxicated.

In addition to boundary shifts, a second problem seen in the clinical setting is that the boundary between the spousal and parental subsystems eventually becomes too diffuse or too rigid. When the boundary is too diffuse and spouses are not clearly distinguishing the functions of parental and spousal systems, whatever goes wrong in one arena is felt keenly in the other. For instance, in a family where a child is caught stealing, the mother and father may become angry with each other rather than directing their energies toward dealing constructively with the child. The reverse also might happen, where spousal quarreling is directed onto the children, who are punished or disciplined for ordinary behavior. This diffuse boundary amplifies problems through both subsystems. The alcoholic copes by drinking more, the co-dependent spouse copes by rigidly clinging to the family structure with its diffuse boundaries and children support the structure by maintaining their position in it.

Clinically, it is seen that the boundary between the spousal and parental subsystems can also become too rigid, so that communication about spousal and parental functions is restricted. As an alcoholic father avoids parental functions and communication between the wife and husband concerning parenting is restricted, the father may become disengaged as a spouse. As mentioned before, when one family member is disengaged, it takes an increasingly extreme situation to provoke contact or a response from the disengaged family member. Family members then come to rely on providing crises to establish contact with each other. When the family system contains children who can perform this function in addition to the mother, the system provides dad with more crises. In fact, the presence of children may intensify the problems of the alcoholic parent by forcing him/her to recognize his/her parenting failures at times of crisis (Downs, 1982).

THE EFFECT OF THE PARENTAL SUBSYSTEM
ON THE SIBLING SUBSYSTEM

The previous sections have drawn a picture of two impaired parents, not just one. The alcoholic parent is impaired through the debilitating use of alcohol. The non-alcoholic parent is impaired through the stress of trying to cope with an alcoholic situation and the stress resulting from trying harder and harder to use solutions which end up making the situation worse (Mendenhall, 1986). The strongest support for the idea that family dysfunction may be both a cause and an effect of alcoholism is inferred from the literature concerning the impact of alcoholism on children. The same interactional patterns which have been traced from the spousal subsystem to the parental subsystem appear to be present in the sibling subsystem. Parental conflict is a dominant theme in literature on children of alcoholics (Wilson, 1982), and the hostility pattern seen in the children is clear. Literature reviews report that children of alcoholics have higher social aggression, more anti-social behavior (Jacob et al., 1978), more temper tantrums, an abnormal amount of dissension among brothers and sisters (Wilson, 1982), more trouble at school, more fights with peers (Jacob et al., 1978), greater delinquency (Jacob et al., 1978; Wilson, 1982), and resentment towards parents (Booz, Allen, and Hamilton, Inc., 1974). One review reported that 50% of children of alcoholics said they were constantly angry with their parents (Gorad, 1971).

Reviews also indicate that children participate in safeguarding and protecting, previously mentioned as spousal coping styles. Children intervene as peacemakers, tidy up, attend to injuries, and stay home to prevent fights and protect parents (Umana, Gross, and McConville, 1981). Additionally, the withdrawal spousal coping style seems to be reflected in children's functioning. Reviews show some children of alcoholics are more likely to evade unpleasantness (Jacob et al., 1978), have difficulty making or keeping close relationships with peers (Wilson, 1982), be isolated socially (Jacob et al., 1978), run away (Jacob et al., 1978; Van Houten, 1978) or leave home prematurely to marry or to have children (Jacob et al., 1978). One review reported that 30% of the children of alcoholics became depressed and passive (Gorad, 1971). These findings indicate that the patterns of withdrawal and disengagement, first seen in the spousal subsystem, are conveyed to and utilized by the sibling subsystem. The sobriety-intoxication pattern, cited by Steinglass (1982), has been suggested as a source of confusion, unpredictability and chaos in the family, contributing to family dysfunction. Ninety percent of alcoholics' children surveyed in one study indicated that their parents' behavior was unpredictable (Gorad, 1971). Several reviews report that children of alcoholics suffer lower self-esteem, security and sense of trust, due to parent unpredictability and inconsistency (Gorad, 1971; Jacob et al., 1978; Morehouse and Richards, 1983).

Reports from children of alcoholics also suggest difficulties in familial subsystem boundaries. Younger children have been found to resent older children's parental authority (Wilson, 1982). Children of alcoholics take a large measure of responsibility for household tasks, assume a large share of child care, and feel overburdened (Booz, Allen, and Hamilton, Inc., 1974; Gorad, 1971; Wilson 1982). These results indicate children have crossed over the parental subsystem boundary. These children also report that they perceive less parental attention and affection (Gorad, 1971), perhaps indicating parental disengagement.

The consequences experienced by an alcoholic's children also become active forces in the family life. Trouble at school, delinquency, holding resentments, and staying home from school, for example, have an impact on the parental subsystem. Co-dependent spouses, who already have many stresses to contend with, have to manage children's hostility and try to shield them from the family problems (Jacob and Seilhamer, 1982). The spouse's ability or inability to cope with the alcoholic situation and its attending circumstances may prove to be even more an influence on family life than spousal drinking. Guebaly and Orford (1977) found that children who had alcoholic fathers but who had high emotional satisfaction with mothers showed positive social behavior. A reasonable conclusion would be that children who are delinquent, in trouble at school, and frequently angry are not going to have high emotional satisfaction with mothers. Another reasonable conclusion would be that children who are helpful, try to alleviate mother's stress, and help take over responsibilities—the hero role that Wegscheider (1981) postulates—will have higher emotional satisfaction with their mothers and help reduce family stress rather than contribute to it.

The previous discussion of subsystem boundaries included the notion that the more rigid the boundaries between subsystems, the more restricted the communication across subsystems and consequently the more extreme crisis is needed to provoke contact across boundaries. It might be hypothesized that children who get into trouble are responding to parental disengagement and have to provoke extreme crisis in order to have contact with them. Of course, the effect of these crises on the already dysfunctional system may further amplify the problems.

It also might be hypothesized that children who stay home from school, who tidy up and take care of parents may be indicating their active participation in an enmeshed system where the boundaries are too diffuse, where parental, spousal, and sibling functions are all intertwined. In this instance, children may help maintain or increase alcoholic behavior and co-dependent behavior by shielding parents from the natural consequences of their behavior.

As children impact the parental subsystem, whatever rules and patterns are in effect will impact the spousal system. For instance, a son gets into trouble at school, finding it the only way he can establish contact with his emotionally disengaged parents. If the mother gets angry with the father, not the son, the son's behavior has impacted the spousal subsystem, and a bigger crisis may be needed to direct the parents' attention to the son.

Finally, although not considered here, the complexities within the sibling subsystem may have an effect on the interactional patterns developed and the boundaries surrounding subsystems. For instance, Wegscheider (1981) suggests that as each new child enters the sibling subsystem, a different role or patterned behavior is adopted by each, a role that will help to maintain the alcoholism by somehow shielding the alcoholic from his natural consequences. Interestingly enough, these roles (hero, scapegoat, lost child, mascot) correspond fairly closely to the patterns of hostility, withdrawal, and protection mentioned throughout this paper.

CONCLUSION

Much of the confusion in the alcoholism field stems from its struggle with language, with confusion in terminology (Mendenhall, 1986). The language used when talking about the impact of alcohol on families has supported the perspective that the alcoholic is actively engaged in impacting his/her family while the rest of the family members are helpless, inactive victims. By making separate distinctions between family subsystems, the effect of alcohol on each subsystem, and vice versa, can be seen. The mediating effects of family interactional patterns across subsystems and consequently on alcohol use become more clear, and some basic patterns emerge. One result of this changed focus is the recognition of the role of the active co-dependent and its subsequent effect on the alcoholic and the rest of the family. While many professionals may want to view alcoholism and its effects from a systemic view, they have been hindered by a lack of systemic language. The family systems concepts of *patterned behavior* and *family structure* seem to provide that language and viewpoint which can help build a stronger understanding of the interaction between alcoholism and family functioning.

REFERENCES

Booz, Allen & Hamilton, Inc. (1974). An assessment of the needs and resources for children of alcoholic parents. National Institute on Alcohol Abuse and Alcoholism.

Cork, R. H. (1969). *The forgotten children*. Alcoholism and Drug Addiction Research Foundation of Ontario, Toronto, Ontario.

Downs, W. R. (1982). Alcoholism as a developing family crisis. *Family Relations, 31*, 5-12.

Gorad, S. L. (1971). Communicational styles and interaction of alcoholics and their wives. *Family Process, 10*, 475-480.

Guebaly, N., & Orford, D. R. (1977). The offspring of alcoholics: a critical review. *American Journal of Psychiatry, 134*, 357-365.

Jackson, D. D. (1967). Aspects of conjoint family therapy. In G. H. Zuk & I. Boszormenyi-Nagy (Eds.), *Family Therapy and Disturbed Families* (pp. 28-40). Palo Alto: Science and Behavior Books, Inc.

Jackson, J. K. (1954). The adjustment of the family to the crisis of alcoholism. *Quarterly Journal of Studies on Alcohol, 15*, 562-586.

Jacob, T., Favorini, A., Meisel, A., & Anderson, C. (1978). The alcoholic spouse, children and family interactions: substantive findings and methodological issues. *Journal of Studies on Alcohol, 39*, 1231-1251.

Jacob, T., Ritchey, P., Cvitkovic, J. F., & Blane, H. T. (1981). Communication styles of alcoholic and non-alcoholic families when drinking and non drinking. *Journal of Studies on Alcohol, 42*, 466-482.

Jacob, T., & Seilhamer, R. (1982). The impact on spouses and how they cope. In J. Orford & J. Harwin (Eds.), *Alcohol and the Family* (pp. 114-126). New York: St. Martin's Press.

James, T., & Goldman, M. (1971). Behavior trends of wives of alcoholics. *Quarterly Journal of Studies on Alcohol, 32*, 373-381.

Lemert, E. M. (1960). The occurrence and sequence of events in adjustment of families to alcohol. *Quarterly Journal of Studies on Alcohol, 21*, 679-697.

Mendenhall, W. (1986). Dynamics of Co-Dependency. Unpublished manuscript.

Minuchin, S. (1974). *Families and family therapy*. Cambridge, Mass.: Harvard University Press.

Morehouse, E. R., & Richards, T. (1983). An examination of dysfunctional latency age children of alcoholic parents and problems in intervention. In M. Frank (Ed.), *Children of Exceptional Parents* (pp. 21-33). New York: The Haworth Press.

Orford, J., & Guthrie, S. (1976). Coping behavior used by wives of alcoholics: a preliminary investigation. In G. Edward, R. D. Hawks, & M. MacCafferty (Eds.), *Alcohol Dependence and Smoking Behavior* (pp. 136-143). Lexington, Mass.: Lexington Books.

Orford, J., Guthrie, S., Nicholls, P., Oppenheimer, E., Egert, S., & Hensman,

C. (1975). Self reported coping behavior of wives of alcoholics and its association with drinking outcome. *Journal of Studies on Alcohol, 36,* 1254-1267.

Steinglass, P. (1982). The roles of alcohol in family systems. In J. Orford & J. Harwin (Eds.), *Alcohol and the Family* (pp. 127-150). New York: St. Martin's Press.

Umana, R. F., Gross, S. J., & McConville, M. T. (1981). *Crisis in the family: three approaches.* New York: Gardner Press.

Van Houten, T. (1978). Adolescent life stress as a predictor of alcohol abuse. National Youth Alternatives Project, Washington, D.C.

Wegscheider, S. (1981). *Another chance.* Palo Alto: Science and Behavior Books, Inc.

Wilson, C. (1982). The impact on children. In J. Orford & J. Harwin (Eds.), *Alcohol and the Family* (pp. 151-166). New York: St. Martin's Press.

Co-dependency Treatment

Warner Mendenhall, PhD

Those individuals most responsible for raising my consciousness about the phenomena of co-dependency were members of A.A. who come to my office to share their lives. These individuals for the most part remained abstinent, went to meetings regularly, worked a good program and were still waiting for things to get better. Another group, spouses of alcoholics, was complaining about the limited relief gained from sobriety alone. The common ground shared by these people was that they came from families of origin in which they had been conditioned to adapt to abnormal behavior. These behavioral abnormalities originated perhaps three generations earlier. The major response by the individuals to this abnormal situation was to develop a coping mechanism best described as dysfunctional dependency or co-dependency. What became clear is that dysfunction dependencies are a transgenerational phenomena. The irrational family rules and beliefs, once developed in response to the addictive behavior, persist across multigenerations and may evolve into a condition having little to do with drinking/addiction per se. Of course, alcoholism is a destructive force for the individual or family, but the patterns of dysfunctional dependencies or co-dependency are even more destructive and insidious. In spite of our best efforts and some success in putting out the brush fire of addiction, the forest fire of co-dependency is raging and spreading from generation to generation, perpetuating a ripe environment for suffering and addiction.

Before proceeding with a clinical paradigm for recovery from dysfunctional dependencies, a review of the characteristics of this

---

Warner Mendenhall is Professor, Wayne College, University of Akron, Akron, OH, and is in psychotherapy practice in Canton, OH.

dysfunctional family is necessary. In whatever generation the addiction began, the orientation of the addictive parent was that they were defensive, negative, fearful, manipulative, promise breakers, liars, blamers, withdrawn, pretenders, resentful, confused, self-destructive, unpredictable, drunk, abusive, violent, depressed, moody, suspicious, demanding, compulsive, critical, impulsive, perfectionists, arrogant, sarcastic, selfish, self-centered, lazy and alcohol focused. Moreover, they misidentified problems, made crazy rules, passed the buck, had poor intimate relationships, were unable to plan, unwilling to re-evaluate decisions, were emotionally not at home and were given to hiding, isolation and ignoring others. This is the same parent who could be loving, generous, supportive and caring without alcohol. This disease also takes over the life of the nonalcoholic parent. The nondrinking spouse who used to help the children with their homework and genuinely care about themselves and others becomes self-righteous, controlling, withdrawn, silent, nervous, self-hating, critical, dishonest, indulgent, lonely, frightened, passive, violent, indirect, contrasting, pretending, fake, depressed, unassertive, approval seeking, phony, preoccupied, denying, liar, confused, despondent, unable to communicate and fearful. Additionally, they felt guilty, had a poor sexual self-image, were frustrated, escaped into workaholism, were in poor health, were self-centered but other focused.

More descriptive terms could be added to each list but certainly this review is sufficient to make clear that anyone who learns to adjust to the environment presented in an addictive family system must adopt maladaptive behavior in order to survive. These behaviors are, of course, continued in adult life and constitute the continuing rich environment for further dysfunction or addiction. It is clear that both alcoholics and nonalcoholics are victims of this pattern of dysfunction dependencies. From my clinical practice, it has become clear that most members of A.A. are co-dependent.

To make the implied explicit, the list of people who suffer from this dysfunctional pattern of co-dependency includes:

1. A person, alcoholic, or nonalcoholic who had an alcohol or drug dependent parent.

2. A person, alcoholic, or nonalcoholic who had a co-dependent parent.
3. A person, alcoholic, or nonalcoholic who has an addicted spouse.
4. A person, alcoholic, or nonalcoholic who has an addicted child.
5. A person, alcoholic, or nonalcoholic who has a co-dependent spouse.
6. A person, alcoholic, or nonalcoholic who has a co-dependent or addicted grandparent because these rules and beliefs are truly multigenerational.

The design of this paper is to provide a clinical working paradigm that has proven useful in working with alcoholics and nonalcoholics alike who are suffering from the dysfunctional dependencies of co-dependency. I will present eleven issues that persistently present as the main areas of recovery.

It is critical that any treatment design is to get the person to acknowledge their own situation – their own reality. This is usually a slow task of emerging awareness for it is hard to recognize that you have actually been in a family that has been dysfunctioned due to the application of a few narrow rules, rigid beliefs and limiting patterns of behavior. To really get the person to accept the generic, biological and psychological vulnerability of this situation is the essential beginning. As people make this connection, of course, feeling will follow. Their feelings will range from relief, hope, joy, grief and guilt; and each of these must be placed in perspective before actual treatment for recovery can begin.

The first issue is control. Co-dependents have not learned that we have control over what we think and feel – that they have absolute and exclusive domain over their inside world. For the person who becomes co-dependent in childhood, there has been no opportunity to experience this kind of self-centered control. The main reason child psychiatrists insist on the need of constancy in a child's world is because they need to learn how to effect their world. A child feels in control of self if they have a consistent effect on their world. If you grow up in an alcoholic home where little is consistent, the child is unable to experience a consistent effect. They come to believe as they grow up that the solution to their feeling of no control can be lessened if they control their environment. The child is only capable of concluding that if there is something wrong in their world, they are responsible and if they cannot figure out what to do differently to get the desired response for themselves, they had best learn how to control the responders (others). Somehow in this switch the child assumes that if they control others they will get what they needed as children. So in the adult years, the feeling of being in control moves from having a consistent effect on one's world to being in control of others. For those persons who experience the onset of co-dependency in later life, a similar problem emerges. As the addiction progresses, the uncertainties and inconsistencies increase; and with blame and guilt, the adult comes to live an emotional life built on fear of abandonment and failure. As explained in an earlier chapter, the adult using the normal culturally approved ways of helping a sick family member cannot figure out what is going wrong so they assume the responsibility for things not working and insist on trying harder to do the things that are not working.

These families' dysfunction is experienced by the presence of unclear and uncertain personal boundaries. These families' communication increases, there is heightened sensitivity and boundaries become blurred. When a person is unclear about their own boundaries, they try to control others in order to feel safe. In doing this, everyone gets into everyone else's physical and emotional space. All family members become hypervigilant and super alert to what is going on inside other family members. Each person tries to control the environment so as not to lose control of self.

Frequently, this control is attempted by a barrage of language which reveals nothing but intrudes into the private boundaries of all other family members. Other people control by not answering the phone, not listening or talking too much or simply not being available to talk. Some people control by keeping their spouse drinking. If my spouse is drunk, I can look better to the children and neighbors and be in control. Some people control by being overprepared. Others control by being sure that everybody around believes and feels as they do. Frequently, people control by discouraging others from having feelings. Without relief from this need to control, the person becomes a candidate for subsurface panic. The stress and strain of unexpected change simply becomes too threatening. Frequently, this stress becomes somatized and constitutes one of the major reasons we see so many co-dependents with physical health problems. The person who needs to control comes to anticipate the worst possible alternative which usually does not come true, but our internal systems don't know if it is true or not; they just respond to the panic. For the person who needs to control, everything is seen as having the optimum effect and hence the subsurface panic becomes a constant feeling for the co-dependent.

The co-dependent person must be helped to see that a new life can only be achieved by letting go of what we cannot control. This will happen if they come to understand and feel that serenity is possible through changes in their thinking and not change by controlling another. In other words, to control thinking and feeling rather than others is a goal of recovery therapy. Clearly, peace of mind is the due of each human; but it will elude the person who is trapped by a desire to direct another's step. Any efforts on fantasy of controlling others is wasted and arrests the need for personal growth. Co-dependents must learn that strength is in centeredness and not in control of others.

The very foundation of our ability to fulfill our functions as human beings is trust — trust in ourselves, others, the world and God. The second major goal in co-dependency treatment is the restoration of self-trust. Frequently, people complain about not being able to trust others when, in fact, the real issue is not being able to trust themselves. Once a person trusts themselves, they can generalize this trust to other areas. The co-dependent has learned to not trust self as they have learned that their feelings do not matter. They conclude that if my feelings are not important, how can I be important? The reality is that the co-dependent cannot trust others but can trust self even less. Remember that the child growing up with a parent suffering from addictive disease is growing up in an environment of contradiction. The child can never learn what makes a difference because if a child behaves the same way, he/she rarely gets the same reaction. If responses are inconsistent, the child can never figure out how to behave. So very early the child learns that they cannot take care of themselves and if they cannot take care of themselves, they certainly cannot trust themselves. As a child repeatedly goes through this pattern, they conclude that either their central nervous system is lying or a parent is lying. Since children unreservedly adore their parents, the inescapable conclusion is that the adult response is correct and in order to survive, the child must ignore their own central nervous system. So a child comes to distrust their feelings and when you do that, you come to not trust yourself.

An example of such a contradiction comes from a story told by a patient. He remembered the Christmas that Mom did not come down to get her presents or watch her children open theirs. The father said nothing about the absence of the mother and simply went ahead with Christmas as if nothing was wrong. The patient knew that something was wrong; but since Dad was pretending otherwise, the child had no choice but to subscribe to his father's behavior. Living with such contradiction between what is sensed and what is acknowledged is the same for the adult who is living with an addictive disease. This person senses that something is wrong but is told either that it isn't so or to ignore. Not only do co-dependents not get an explanation of the event, but they are also told that what they see is really not there. If this is a constant message, the person comes to disbelieve themselves and that means distrust of one's own sensory perceptions. If you cannot trust your feelings, why bother to have them? The co-dependent must be encouraged to stop living the lie told them by others and believed by them. The lie told and believed is that the co-dependent does not know what they know nor feel what they feel. In this atmosphere the co-dependent learns to stay outside of themselves in order to keep the relationship in place. This, of course, can only be done if the co-dependent becomes overresponsible. For the co-dependent to see more honestly what is going wrong would require recognition of the self as dysfunctional and in order to avoid that conclusion, the co-dependent attempts to normalize and maintain the situation — "After all, it's not that bad."

The third issue in this treatment paradigm is the issue of overresponsibility. The task here is to help the person avoid being superresponsible. This overresponsibility can develop in the child or in the adult. For the child who up to the age of eight can only see themselves as the center of the universe, it is natural for this problem to develop. If children see themselves as the center of what happens, they feel responsible and believe that they caused it. For the small child, everything becomes "my fault" because they are unable to separate their part of a situation from the parents' part. Moreover, the children, unlike adults, have nothing with which to compare their present circumstances. So the children conclude: whatever is going on, I caused it; and if I caused it, I need to fix it.

For the adult, the dysfunction caused by alcohol or drug usage leads automatically to overresponsibility — the overresponsibility of necessity. As the drug-affected person gets worse — withdrawn, inconsistent, inconsiderate, abusive and neglectful — the nonusing spouse takes on more and more of the family function — paying the bills, earning a living, shopping, P.T.A., laundry, mothering, fathering, disciplining the children, cleaning, picking up, repairing, cutting the grass, helping with homework. This person comes to feel that if I don't do it, it won't get done and, of course, it has to be done. The feeling is I am all alone, and I must do it all. This is, of course, exasperated by the drug-affected person who by isolation and criticism puts enormous pressure on the nonusing spouse to assume all the responsibility. When you feel responsible for everything, you are overresponsible. In the most extreme form, this means that the co-dependent takes on the responsibility for the feelings of others. In the extreme form, the co-dependent comes to sincerely believe that if they can just get their spouse or parent to feel toward them the way they need to have them feel, then, and only then, will they feel O.K. about themselves. In this dual approach, the co-dependent is both driven to control and consumed with overresponsibility.

The fourth task in recovery is to help people recognize their emotional indigency. Co-dependents learn to avoid feelings. As children grow up in an addictive family, they learn that having feelings can get them into trouble and that if they express their feelings, they will be ignored. The child has also learned that if the drug-dependent person is anxious, they can get hurt. In adult life, if a person expresses themselves, they get contradicted or ignored. In both the child and the adult, the interaction with the drug-dependent person provides a confusing context in which to exist. In that environment, the co-dependent never knows how feelings are going to be received. Such uncertainty leads to the co-dependent becoming more concerned with the reaction of others than they are about expressing their own feelings. Most co-dependents in the depths of dependency can only respond when asked about their feelings that they are confused. Their stated confusion is usually some blend of guilt, anger, hurt, inadequacy, fear and loneliness. It becomes essential for survival for the co-dependent to stay away from feeling so they avoid talking to or being around people who might relate at the feeling level. The co-dependent comes to avoid listening, reading, movies, or music that might evoke feelings. Hence, they become isolated and are frozen in their ability to feel. Co-dependents must learn to feel the way they would feel if they already had that feeling.

The fifth area of recovery requires the co-dependent person to reconnect feeling and experience, as well as thinking and feeling. As a child or adult realizes that in order to survive they cannot have feeling, they must separate or disassociate feelings from behavior. This disassociation results in the inability to make the connection between feeling and doing. This disassociation of feelings from behavior makes sense because it enables the child to survive in an inconsistent, arbitrary, unpredictable, chaotic environment. Remember that the child concludes that this crazy environment is their fault and that they must do something to prevent its continuation. So the adjustment the child makes is to pull themselves apart from their feelings. If an adult is being blatantly ignored or contradicted by their spouse, the same pattern emerges. The discordancy between what a person feels and the denial of that feeling by significant family members leads to disassociation in order to survive. The natural way for an adult to try to make sense of their world is to separate their world into a private feeling world and a public behaving world. For the child and the adult, behavior cannot be based on their feelings but on the behavioral expectations of others. Survival requires disassociation. Many co-dependents have internalized the coercion to such an extent that they must be taught how to search for their own awareness else they remain victims of repetitive compulsion which always results from a separation of feeling from experience.

The sixth step in co-dependency recovery requires the person to recognize their personal needs. As co-dependency develops, the person increasingly puts their personal needs aside. When a child asks for something like help me tie my shoe, tuck me into bed, or help me with my homework, the most favorable response is I love you but leave me alone. The message is clear — something else is more important. Of course, sometimes this is true; but when it becomes the dominant message, the child comes to know that their needs are not very important. If a child has a need and expresses it, they are in a real bind — to try to get the need met means they run the risk of learning once again how unimportant they really are.

For the adult, the situation is much the same. If the co-dependent has a need and the spouse either denies it or ignores it, the co-dependent is in a real one-down position. To have a need is to give to another person the power to tell the co-dependent that they are worthless. So rather than let the spouse tell the co-dependent they don't count, it is easier to not have a need. It is easier to say I don't need than to hear how unimportant you are. For the adult, this situation becomes even more serious. If someone else has a need, the co-dependent must satisfy that need because the co-dependent doesn't even dare have a need to not respond to the other person's need. In the extreme, the co-dependent comes to do first what others expect even to the point of serious jeopardy of their physical health. Co-dependents especially experience problems of hypertension, colitis, bowel problems, anxiety, hypochondria, depression, insomnia, asthma, cardiac irregularities, respiratory disease and inadequate sexual performance.

The next treatment area requires the person to learn moderation. Co-dependents come to be extremely immoderate. In addictive families, the child learns that only the extreme gets attention. Normal needs or low-level complaints are ignored. Even if the child gets terribly upset there is often no one to respond because the adults are preoccupied. The only chance the child has to get a response is to act in the extreme. In adulthood, life experienced only in the extreme leaves the person with few alternatives — black or white; true or false; all right or all wrong; success or failure; or doing everything or doing nothing. Since no one is always successful, this type of internal equation of immoderation means that the person experiences a lot of failure. The co-dependents need to be taught that it is okay to be okay, that it is okay to be fine, that it is okay to let it slide and that it is okay to just get by. What has previously been black and white must become color.

The eighth element in co-dependency recovery is the need to recognize flashbacks. Another label for this phenomenon is unconscious age regression. Not all age regression is bad because it enables us to dance, play and have fun, but the way the process works in co-dependency is harmful. When a co-dependent experiences a feeling, they unconsciously flash back in their memory to their experience with that feeling in the past. Moreover, the co-dependent not only picks up the past feeling, but also picks up the level of coping skills that existed around that feeling in past time. For the child, the family context has interfered with the development of any effective coping mechanism. For the adult, almost all efforts at coping have failed. The result is that the co-dependent experiences at the conscious level the feeling of inadequate coping skill and concludes that they are helpless. The age regression happens at the unconscious level, but the inability to cope is perceived at the conscious level. The co-dependent must be taught this connection so that they are free to respond with present day coping skills rather than being trapped by their past.

The ninth step in co-dependency recovery is the unraveling of the confused feeling state. The feelings are confused because as a family becomes more dysfunctional, the console of feeling grows more limited. The number of available feelings frequently degenerates to one — anger. When a person has only a few feelings available, it means that a lot of other feelings are subsumed under those few and there is frequent mislabeling of feeling as well as confusion about those feelings. Typically, the co-dependent will confuse sadness with depression, intensity with intimacy, obsession with care, and control for security. The co-dependent comes to believe that if they are criticized they are not loved; that if you let me take care of you then you love me; that caring about is caring for. Furthermore, co-dependents frequently believe that if they are feeling calm they must be depressed, if assertive they must be aggressive, if having fun then they must be irresponsible. The co-dependent skips from a healthy feeling to an unhealthy one without conscious recognition.

As the co-dependent's console of feeling shrinks, so also does their way of relating to others. The tenth step is the restoration of multiple patterns of relationships. As a family becomes increasingly dysfunctional, the response set becomes very limited. Typically a dysfunction family will only manage to display one or two interactional patterns. As with feelings, relationships become distorted and camouflaged. Co-dependents are unable to know how to relate, how to talk or how to be a friend. They don't even know that having a friend is an option.

The final step in recovery is to help co-dependents draw up a bill of rights for themselves. This needs to be an itemized list of what each human deserves as a condition of life. Usually co-dependents have such a list which they use to determine other people's rights but have never included themselves among those who deserve the same treatment. To get the co-dependent to treat themselves as they believe others should be treated is a necessary step in treatment for co-dependency.

Clearly, each therapist will want to add other items to this modality of recovery and many would be useful in some cases and some would be useful in all cases. This list has not been presented as exhaustive, but it does represent the major areas of a treatment design derived from clinical practices. In closing, one word of caution is necessary. The process of co-dependency recovery is necessarily slow. This process is like learning a foreign language requiring new words, new ways of thinking, new relationships and lots of practice. These steps in recovery must be presented in a deliberate way so that the person can always experience success. Otherwise, the healing process may reaffirm damaging and self-defeating ways of thinking that will themselves become an issue requiring additional therapy. It is helpful to conceive of this process as taking up to three years. The language of wellness requires patience, practice and time on the part of both therapist and patient.

There are six stages of co-dependency recovery. First, there is the period of undoing. This is a painful period because it seems like things are being taken away that still have value. Letting go of the familiar even if it is harmful is a demanding, painful process. During this first stage, the person cherishes the familiar because they cannot yet see the lack of value in the past efforts nor can they conceive of what will take its place. The second stage is a period of gathering and sorting data in order to decide what behaviors are helpful and which are not. This is the period when the previous learning is a real hindrance and a time when the person cannot generalize and will frequently need precise examples of helpful behavior. The third stage is again one of enormous conflict. This period is best characterized as a period of relinquishment — a period of giving up behaviors that have seemed to be desirable. During this period, the co-dependent must overcome the thought of lack and sacrifice what seemingly is his/her own best interest.

The fourth stage is a period of settling down or consolidation. At this point the person begins to see the value of what has been learned and can begin to transfer the learning in one situation to another. The fifth stage is again a troubling one — a period of unsettling anxiety caused by the co-dependent beginning to ask themselves what they really want in every circumstance. This takes months of practice and at the outset, many co-dependents are mystified that it is normal to have a preference, especially when they don't have the slightest idea of what they really want, much less that it is normal to have that want. The final stage of co-dependency recovery is best characterized as a period of achievement, achievement marked by the reality that what gains have been made are not permanent and can be relied upon to be in place for the next crisis and to stay intact in emergency. The new behavior has now become the expected norm and with that realization, peace and serenity emerge.

Today with the knowledge, skill and resources, those in need of help can find that help and recover. Just ten years ago these same people did not know what was wrong nor were there trained and experienced professionals. We are living in a new age: therapists do understand co-dependency, twelve step groups specific to co-dependency are getting started in every community. Thousands of people whose lives used to be characterized by overwork, confusion, inability to parent, and exhausted failed personal relationships now have hope. Persons formerly ignored or defined as neurotic can learn to lead productive, happy and integrated lives.

Recovery for Adult Children of Alcoholics: Education, Support, Psychotherapy

Tarpley M. Richards, LCSW

SUMMARY. COAs are a group of co-dependents who as adults exhibit many emotional and behavioral problems. Damage to a child from parental alcoholism may be mild, moderate or severe. This paper will explore characteristics of the alcoholic home and the varied responses of children reared in this environment. Three categories of problems of the ACOA will be described. These include impairment of self-esteem, failure to establish reasonable concepts of personal responsibility and difficulty in appropriately regulating sexual and aggressive drives. The value of helping the ACOA through education, peer support and psychotherapy will be discussed and illustrated through clinical case material.

Over a ten year period I have struggled to determine how best to serve Adult Children of Alcoholics (ACOAs). As a clinician I specialized in the field of alcoholism in 1971. I witnessed the beginnings of DWI programs, the mushrooming of EAP programs, the concept of alcoholism as a family disease and the coining of co-dependency as a clinical syndrome. Each of these events has given new hope to the field of alcoholism. The alcoholic person and his/her significant others have ample opportunity today to arrest chemical dependency and co-dependency in the early stages, resulting in

Tarpley M. Richards is affiliated with the Center for Adult Children of Alcoholics, 1200 15th Street, NW, Suite 400, Washington, DC 20005.

The author would like to give special thanks to her colleagues and co-founders of the Center for Adult Children of Alcoholics, Washington, DC, Martha K. Tuohey, LCSW, and Patricia E. Petrash, LCSW, for our peer supervision over the past ten years; to Floyd Galler, MD, an esteemed medical/psychiatric consultant; and to Amy Robertson, ACSW, and Judy Barnes, LCSW, who in joining the Center have enabled us to offer a broad range of services to ACOAs.

87

better prospects for personal changes and eventual full recovery. Despite these opportunities, however, family members of alcoholics (COAs or spouses, the majority of whom are also ACOAs) remain very tough to treat.

ACOAs are complex and have a variety of needs to be met. I have tried and discarded, tried and modified, tried and kept interventions that held up over time or clearly did not work. I think I hoped eventually to come up with a program that would work for the ACOA patient. After all, in alcohol treatment programs there is a level of uniformity. This makes sense to me because everyone with alcoholism has the same disease. But I found that attempting to take an alcoholism model (treatment of dependency) and imposing it on ACOAs (treatment of co-dependency) produced disappointing results. Apparently my experience is not unique. I recently read an article by James La Bundy who commented: "Treatment paradigms considered highly effective in treating primary disease alcoholism did not appear transferable to co-dependency."[1]

What I have observed is that ACOAs recover through three general categories of "help": education and information, peer support, and psychotherapy. Not every ACOA utilizes all three of these modalities, nor do the modalities seem to be in any particular order of usefulness. Much depends on what difficulties the ACOA has and how she/he connects to the recovery process. The following vignettes illustrate how varied ACOAs are in their response and how important it is for the clinician to be flexible and attentive to the individuality of each ACOA patient.

MARY

Mary was referred to treatment by an EAP counselor. She was a self referral whose chief complaint was depression. The counselor suspected both Mary's parents were practising alcoholics. Mary was consciously oblivious to this possibility even though she spoke openly about their being "drunk all the time."

Mary was a highly functional worker with a demanding job she handled well. She was married to a man who, educationally and occupationally, was strikingly secondary to her. She had a history of involvement with "disgusting" men and never had any friends throughout her life. She referred to her parents as her best friends.

Actually, her relationship with her parents was based on Mary's caretaking activities of them which clouded intense feelings of abandonment, rage and guilt over hating them.

At the suggestion of the EAP counselor Mary first attended an Al-Anon meeting. She left midway through. She said she felt so upset she thought she would die if she had to sit there one more minute. She could not remember anything about the meeting and what had upset her so much. The counselor had also given Mary a book on ACOAs. Mary's response was horror: "My parents may drink a lot but they are not alcoholics," she said, miffed. To press the issues further seemed fruitless to the counselor. Mary was willing to accept a referral to an individual therapist.

Mary's path to recovery began with psychotherapy. After a year or so in treatment she was able to hear information on alcoholism. She started gradually attending seminars on ACOAs and reading ACOA literature. It was several years, though, before Mary was able to attend another Al-Anon meeting. Without first "growing up" in psychotherapy, Mary was not capable of utilizing peer support. To paraphrase La Bundy, people must experience peering before peer support can be a help.[2] For Mary to recover from damage sustained growing up with alcoholic parents, she needed to utilize all three modalities of recovery: first, psychotherapy; next, information; and finally, peer support.

PEGGY

Peggy is a free-lance writer. Her father was an alcoholic and died of liver cirrhosis. No one in the family ever talked about his drinking. As the years went by the family became more isolated. Peggy excelled in school and was a popular, if infrequent, social friend. When she was 20 she befriended a woman 15 years her senior, fell in love with her and subsequently became involved in a gay life-style. She is now 35 years old. She is happy with her relationship and feels loved and nurtured.

Peggy read an article on COAs ten years ago and has kept up with nearly every COA publication since. She says she is not in pain and has no wish to change her love life, her work, her cordial, if distant, relationships with family and friends. She does say, however, that the reading she has done on COAs has changed her life, in that she has been able to understand many aspects of her family life which were a mystery to her. She finds reading about the experiences of others to provide her with an inner peace she has not known before. She continues to work through her early experiences by including COA issues in her writing, both fiction and non-fiction.

Peggy feels no need for support through peers who are ACOAs, nor is she interested in psychotherapy. Her life is orderly and satisfying and her work is rewarding. She does not appear to be harming herself or others. Her recovery began and continues with information and education on alcoholism and COAs. She made good use of an educational cure.

ARLENE

Arlene is a 45-year-old enthusiastic, outgoing woman who grew up with a practising alcoholic mother. She lived in the "Bible Belt," an area of the United States where drinking is frowned upon and alcoholism in women is still considered morally reprehensible in the community. In the '50s when Arlene was a teenager she was very popular with both girls and boys. She was best friends with several girls and was the "ear" to everyone's problems. She cleverly disguised the fact that although she appeared open because of her humor, sympathy, and receptivity, she never revealed anything personal about herself. This worked for her until she was 31 years old.

About this time, Arlene's mother began to experience severe physical deterioration from alcoholism. Arlene, now married with four children, began to commute 1,000 miles every few months to "get mother squared away." Gradually Arlene developed colitis and ulcers. Her physician, after taking a careful family history, recommended she attend Al-Anon. That was 10 years ago.

Arlene continues to be active in Al-Anon. She always had friends. In Al-Anon she learned how to share herself both with other Al-Anon members and with the friends to whom she had been such a support and comfort over the years. Through Al-Anon she learned mutuality and interdependence in relationships. She continues to have a good marriage and her children are healthy and stable.

Arlene has never read a book on ACOAs. She has not attended

specialized ACOA/Al-Anon meetings. She has not been in psycho-therapy. She never denied her mother's alcoholism; somehow she overcame her shame enough so that she could engage in supportive peer relationships and establish a trusting, loving relationship with a man. Al-Anon helped Arlene sort out appropriate responsibilities and allowed her cathartic experiences. She feels satisfied with her continuing recovery.

Many books have been written on the traits ACOAs share. Point-ing out commonalities is very important because this validates that the environment in the alcoholic home is damaging to the well-being of children. However, where "help" and "how to recover from the experience" is concerned, differences in ACOAs must be taken into consideration. In terms of adult life problems, a "family hero" and a "scapegoat"[3] are likely to have little in common. The hero will more often than not be president of a corporation while the scapegoat may be in prison.

In evaluating the ACOA clinically, one needs to go beyond de-scription. For example, that COAs have impaired self-esteem has been well addressed by Black and Woititz.[4,5] Behaviorally, low self-esteem can be expressed in disparate ways: isolation from peers, chaotic lifestyle, sado-masochistic relationships and compulsive over achievement. Each of these expressions of low self-esteem requires a different remedy. A person who has spent a lifetime in relative isolation would probably not follow a suggestion to attend an Al-Anon meeting. Placing a chaotic person in an ACOA group would likely serve only to blow the group apart.[6]

This paper will address the varying impact an alcoholic parent may have on the child and will focus specifically on how education, peer support, and/or psychotherapy serve the difference between as well as the commonalities among ACOAs.

PARENTING IMPAIRMENT RESULTING FROM ALCOHOLISM IN THE FAMILY

Parental alcoholism has an impact on children. The characteris-tics of the alcoholic home should be viewed on a continuum. In order to qualify as an alcoholic home, there must be some of the characteristics present. The *degree* to which the characteristic is present is the variable.

Parental role instability. An intoxicated parent cannot fulfill parental responsibilities. In some homes intoxication is continuous and the alcoholic loses all ability to function as a parent. In other families the alcoholic binges; the parent may function admirably for several months only to go on a binge and drop out of sight. In still other families, intoxication is a rare event. The parent sort of muddles along, functioning marginally.

Parental undependability. The alcoholic parent may be consistently unreliable, intermittently unreliable or unexpectedly and perplexibly unreliable.

Environmental chaos. The level of chaos in an alcoholic family may range from crisis management of the homelife (searching for reservations for dinner at 3 pm on Christmas day because mother, drunk, burned up the turkey) to daily acts of terror (slapping, screaming, slamming doors, phones ripped out of walls).

Emotional unavailability. Alcoholism produces an increasing self-centeredness in the drinker as well as the co-dependent spouse. This self-centeredness, translated into neglect of children's needs, may be mild, severe or extreme, depending upon the rapidity of the progression of the illness.

In addition to the behavior of the alcoholic and the co-alcoholic, there are other variables which influence the impact of alcoholism on the child.[7]

The sex of the alcoholic parent. Research on COAs indicates that when the mother is alcoholic, the damage to the child is worse.[8] Having two alcoholic parents is correlated with severe psychological damage and susceptibility to the development of alcoholism in the teen years.[9]

The sex of the child. Boys appear to be more vulnerable to adverse effects from parental alcoholism than are girls.[9]

The age of the child at the onset of alcoholism in the parent. The unborn child is at risk for fetal alcohol syndrome if the mother is alcoholic. Damage is greater the younger the child is when parental alcoholism begins.[10]

The specific manifestations of the drinking behavior. Chaotic homes have a tendency to produce chaotic children or children who are rigid and inflexible. Some alcoholics are able to protect their families and to harm only themselves seriously. Families which preserve a high degree of cohesiveness despite the drinking of an alcoholic parent appear to suffer less.[11]

The attitude of the non-alcoholic parent. In families where the non-alcoholic spouse is severely co-dependent (i.e., denies the drinking is a problem, is withdrawn, isolated, refuses Al-Anon or other help) the children are likely to have major problems. In other families where the non-alcoholic parent actively fights the compelling draw of co-dependency (i.e., acknowledges the problem, holds the alcoholic accountable for his/her actions, maintains friends, protects children, seeks help) the children have a better chance to escape damages to their reality testing and sociability.

The availability of other adult role models. This may be either inside or outside the family. Isolation is the hallmark of the alcoholic family. Children who are fortunate to have other relatives, concerned church members or neighbors who step in and provide needed support may avoid the permanent scarring of early deprivation.

The specific personality of the child. Some children who endure depriving early years do become adaptable, competent, relatively content adults. Other children are devastated by the experience and struggle continually to adjust to adult life. It is the specific ACOA personality who arrives at an Al-Anon meeting, attends a conference on ACOAs, picks up a copy of the several popular books on COAs. Each ACOA grew up with parental alcoholism. But how each perceived the experience, internalized it, defended against it is particularly unique.

RESPONSES OF THE CHILD GROWING UP IN AN ALCOHOLIC FAMILY

In the previous section I spoke of specific parenting impairment in the alcoholic home. Figure 1 depicts frequent responses of chil-

RESPONSES OF THE CHILD GROWING UP IN AN ALCOHOLIC FAMILY

* pseudomaturity (unclear personal responsibility)

* "people pleasing" (unclear personal responsibility)

* compulsive overachievement (self-esteem)

* difficulty leaving home (unclear personal responsibility)

* controlling behaviors (drives)

* attachment to chaos (drives)

* inability to have fun (drives)

* high tolerance for unacceptable behavior (self esteem)

PARENTAL ROLE INSTABILITY

ENVIRONMENTAL CHAOS

PARENTAL UNDEPENDABILITY

EMOTIONAL UNAVAILIBILITY

* low tolerance for feelings of loss, anger and disappointment (drives)

* turning passive (victim) into active (identification with the aggressor) (drives)

* feigned indifference in relationships (drives)

* unrealistic expectations of others (unclear personal responsibility)

* hesitancy about physical intimacy (drives)

* fear of abandonment and/or engulfment in relationships (drives)

Figure 1

dren to these parenting deficits.* The responses are described behaviorally, that is, the clinician and the patient can point to specific
examples of the problems the ACOA is experiencing. The responses are further categorized into one of three headings for the
benefit of the clinician who is in the position of recommending
therapy, support or education to the ACOA. The categories are:

• poor self-esteem
• unclear personal responsibility
• impairment in the regulation of the instinctual drives, sex and
  aggression

Poor self-esteem arises from thoughts and feelings a person has
which she/he considers unacceptable. ACOAs are usually painfully
aware of shame, embarrassment and guilt. It is the guilt which bat-
ters self-esteem, for behind the guilt are intensely angry, hateful
and destructive feelings toward the parents who have so disap-
pointed them. Often these intense unacceptable feelings are unconscious. The patient is only aware of crippling guilt.

It is not surprising that a substantial number of COAs grow up
with confused notions of personal responsibility. Often they have
repeatedly witnessed other adult family members assume the alcoholic's responsibilities. Exactly who is supposed to do what and for
whom is mysterious. The most extreme example of this I have seen
was a couple I met with for an evaluation. Both had two alcoholic
parents and both had life threatening illnesses. The husband had
diabetes and the wife suffered from a heart ailment. The gist of the
session was:

He: The problem is Gail won't take her medicine.
She: The problem is Harry won't take his insulin. He goes into a
    coma and I have to rush him to the emergency room.

---

*Certainly a major response of COAs is their own alcohol and drug abuse in
adolescence and adulthood. When an ACOA seeks help and alcohol/drug dependency is present, the substance abuse must be treated first. It is recommended that
the chemically dependent ACOA be drug free for a minimum of six months and
well connected to AA or other similar recovery program before specific ACOA
issues are addressed.

He: Gail has already had six surgeries. If I don't force her to take her medication regularly she is going to die.

Obviously, the concept of personal responsibility was foreign to Harry and Gail.

Impairment in regulation of the instinctual drives, sex and aggression, affects many COAs. It is a parent's job to "civilize" children and help them successfully sublimate primitive instincts. Far more often than not, sexual and aggressive impulses are acted out in the alcoholic family. This is because alcohol loosens inhibitions. When the intoxicated alcoholic (and even the co-alcoholic parent) feels like yelling, yelling usually ensues. If the alcoholic feels like hitting, hitting follows. If an intoxicated father becomes aware of erotic interests in his daughter, he is more apt than the non-intoxicated father to act on these feelings. Often in alcoholic homes, acting on impulse is countered during sober times by denial of the presence of any feelings at all. Hence, the "aggression" scale in alcoholic families appears like a fahrenheit thermometer with only two readings: zero degrees (denial) and 212 degrees (murderous rage). Likewise, on the sexual, or love, scale there is either no connection at all to another person or intrusiveness and personal boundary invasion.

The ACOA struggles to one degree or another with keeping self-esteem intact, knowing what is or is not one's responsibility, and appropriate discharge of instinctual drives. In order to alter any of these troubling conditions, one must receive help. What help does the ACOA need? They can benefit from one or a combination of several interventions:

• information (books, workshops, seminars)
• peer support (Al-Anon and other self-help ACOA groups)
• psychotherapy (group and individual)

In order for these interventions, or modalities, to work best, the clinician and patient must be clear about exactly what the ACOA patient's problems are and establish recovery goals. Figure 2 matches the responses of children to specific parenting impairment (see Figure 1) with the recovery modalities just identified. To summarize, education and information are very useful in increasing

RECOVERY FOR ADULT CHILDREN OF ALCOHOLICS

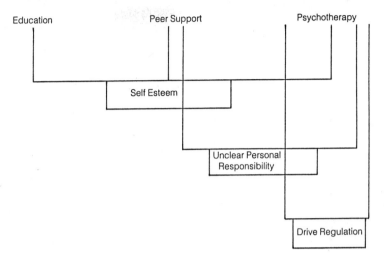

Figure 2

self-esteem. Peer support increases self-esteem and assists the ACOA in clarifying specific questions of personal responsibility. ACOAs can also gain new information and feel support in psycho-therapy; but the chief value of psychotherapy as an intervention is to address disorders of drive regulation and control, which operate unconsciously.

EDUCATION

For many years didactic presentations on the medical and psy-chosocial aspects of alcoholism have been an integral part of most alcoholism treatment programs. Until five years ago, very little was published specifically on the topic of children of alcoholics even though spouses of alcoholics have been studied since the mid '50s. Now there are many excellent articles and books which poignantly describe the impact of alcoholism on children and address the prob-lems COAs experience both as children and, later, adults. In addi-tion to a growing body of literature, there has been an expansion of seminars, workshops and conferences for COAs nationwide. These gatherings are very well attended.

What needs of ACOAs are being met by the rapid expansion of these educational ventures?

Information and education about COAs reduce stigma and provide validation for secret, wrenching emotional experiences. How often I have heard an ACOA say, "Reading this book was like someone had written my life history. I identified with all the problems. I always thought my family was unlike any other in the world. I feel so relieved I am not alone." Clearly, just the knowledge that one's secret is more public and widespread served to heighten self-esteem. Many popular books go further to assure the reader that she/he is entitled to feelings of anger and resentment towards parents. This sort of expert sanction of negative feelings can go far to alleviate the ACOA's guilt for destructive thoughts.

Education about alcoholism and the family can provide a framework for the ACOA to begin to organize thoughts and feelings about current problems she/he is experiencing. Information is neutral and non-threatening in that the reader can take in whatever she/he needs or can tolerate at any given moment. The lecture or conference participant can be passive and even choose to tune out. With information one doesn't have to do anything. And written information, especially, can be filed away and retrieved at a future date. Three years after an article on COAs appeared in the *Washington Post* I still have men and women who come in for an evaluation appointment, pull out their yellowed, tattered newspaper copy and open the session with, "The reason I am here is because I read this and. . . ."

Occasionally education/information is contraindicated. This would occur when the ACOA begins to use information defensively by embarking on search for "more right answers"[12] instead of becoming resigned to the fact that in the final analysis the cure comes from within, not from without. The most difficult, and unsuccessful, case I've ever had in ten years was a woman who from the first interview introduced herself by saying, "I have read every self-help book that has ever been written." Sadly, the more chaotic her life became, the more she read. The chaos continued.

Other then when information is used as a defense, I encourage

ACOAs to read the popular literature and to attend educational lectures. By "encourage" I mean I have order forms for books and announcements for lectures and seminars displayed in my office waiting room. I do not request or require patients to read specific material. As mentioned in one of the vignettes earlier, little is accomplished by asking patients to read books. If they are ready, they will respond to the information in the waiting room; if they are not ready, they will ignore it. What I have discovered is that some patients report ordering books. Others never mention anything about the waiting room fare. The order forms and brochures disappear with great regularity.

PEER SUPPORT

What keeps people comfortable and healthy is support from other human beings. In early childhood, home is one's major support system. As one grows up, gradually peer support supplements or replaces the family as a support. The term support, for adults, is meant to be interpreted as peer relatedness. A hallmark of the alcoholic family is isolation. Isolation means the end of support for these family members since with an active alcoholic and co-dependent there is virtually no support at home and ties with the outside world are broken.

I have always been impressed by the origins of Al-Anon. It was established in the '50s by a group of women married to alcoholic men. Women's support historically has come from other women, informally, over the backyard fence, garden clubs, coffee klatches, etc. Before there was a how-to-do book for every life problem, women, the traditional keepers of family life, dealt with family problems by chatting with other women about everything from preventing diaper rash to stain removal to picky eaters. Everything, that is, except terribly embarrassing things like an alcoholic husband. Alcoholism and its sequellae — abuse, accidents, sexual and financial difficulties probably led these women to self isolate out of the support network. Who can hang out laundry and exchange recipes when one's husband is in withdrawal in the bedroom? The founder of Al-Anon must have understood the need to talk about upsetting home problems with peers: other women who were experiencing the same pain. After AA, Al-Anon was the second organized self-help group in America.

Al-Anon is greeted with mixed reviews by ACOAs. Some of them find Al-Anon a comfort and an enormous help; others find themselves angry that they are asked to relate to the plight of spouses who elected to live with an alcoholic. This latter group of ACOAs maintains they did not choose to grow up in an alcoholic home and as a result their problems are different. It is perhaps this group that was instrumental in the formation of ACOA/Al-Anon groups and other independent ACOA self-help groups. Ironically, many ACOAs drop out of the specialized ACOA meetings and return to general Al-Anon citing "too much negativism" as the reason for quitting ACOA groups and reconnecting with the experience, strength and hope offered by the more traditional organization.

What is most important to recognize is that a substantial number of ACOAs feel helped by belonging to and participating in self-help support groups. Peer support serves to increase self-esteem through openly sharing common life experiences, and as with books, lectures and conferences, support groups provide validation for past torment. In addition, a self-esteem difficulty for ACOAs — high tolerance for unacceptable behavior — can be modified through learning from the experience of others:

> Sue, whose alcoholic mother is still drinking talked in her group about how her Christmas dinner was ruined. "Mother starts drinking in mid-afternoon and is always smashed by 6 o'clock. Dinner was served at 7 and she passed out at the table." Julie then offered, empathetically, "This year we served dinner at one in the afternoon. Then everyone had plans for the evening. My dad got drunk on Christmas day just like he does every other day, but by then everyone had left the house so he couldn't ruin our festivities."
> It had not occurred to Sue that she could do anything other than allow her mother to make her life miserable.

The norm in self-help groups is peer relatedness rather than parent/child symbiosis which is all too common in alcoholic families. The ACOA who confuses self/other responsibilities can make some changes through incorporating the behaviors of healthy role models observed in support groups.

Specific personal responsibility problems which are subject to some modification through self-help are:

- parental child behaviors
- "people pleasing"
- unrealistic expectations of others

Parental Child Behaviors

Beth opened a regular Al-Anon discussion meeting by tonelessly unfolding a story of her parents' incompetence and how she has to make all their decisions for them. After a few minutes, Ruth interjected, "Excuse me, Beth, you are taking your parents' inventory, not your own. In this group our task is to talk about our own thoughts and feelings. We are responsible only for our own behavior. We can't control others."

It had not occurred to Beth that she could not control others behavior. She thought that was her purpose in life.

"People Pleasing"

Sam was a relatively new member of an ACOA Al-Anon group. He arrived early, set up chairs, fixed coffee, and acted as self-appointed host for the attendees. No matter what problem anyone aired, Sam had a comment on how to solve it. After Sam spoke the group became very quiet. Eventually he asked if he said something wrong. Gently Bob commented,

> I know you are trying to be helpful by offering suggestions on how I can solve my problem. I would like it better if you would share experiences from your own life. Have you had a situation like mine? Tell me how you would feel under the circumstances. Letting me know how you feel is the most helpful thing you can do.

Sam was surprised to learn that his taking care of others was not pleasing at all; rather it was irritating to others. He discovered that helping others and being pleasing to them was best accomplished by meeting his own needs first.

Unrealistic Expectations of Others

Gwen confided that she had been in ACOA for a year and had gone through three sponsors. She didn't know what she was doing wrong. Pat replied,

> I ruined my relationship with my first sponsor. I was so thrilled that someone volunteered to listen to me that I literally used her up in no time flat. When she said to call if I was upset, I took that to mean anytime day or night. I called a lot because I was upset a lot. After two weeks she set the limits on the sponsor contract. I was furious. So was she. "Pat," my sponsors said, "You are not an infant on a demand feeding schedule. I have a life too, you know." My next sponsor and I set up a flexible sort of agreement. We meet for lunch weekly and I call her one other time during the week. It works great. I feel taken care of and she doesn't feel taken advantage of."

Gwen was amazed. "Maybe that's the problem. This isn't the first time I've been told I'm too demanding both at home and at work. I never new exactly what that meant. I though it was my tone of voice. Maybe I need to look at what I want from a sponsor and ask up front if the person can or cannot provide it."

PSYCHOTHERAPY

Many ACOAs I have seen for evaluations say they have been in therapy at some point in their lives. When I explore further with them about their experiences in therapy I learn the process "therapy" is used to describe everything from psychoanalysis to primal scream to prayer groups to leaderless groups. There are so many approaches that are included under the rubric of psychotherapy that I need to spell out my definition of this process.

When I use the word psychotherapy I am referring to the application of a skill in addressing unconscious determinants of behavior. Further, to qualify as psychotherapy, the treatment must be provided by a person who has received formal training in one of the legally recognized mental health disciplines and who is accountable to a state licensing committee or a professional ethics board.

There is a bias of informality in helping ACOAs. This is understandable because the visible ACOAs are in AA or Al-Anon groups. AA and Al-Anon thrive on having members who are more advanced in recovery share their personal struggles with neophytes. Also, the hourly meeting is often a springboard to strengthen peer ties outside the group. Pre-meeting chatting and after-meeting socializing are extremely important to the recovery of members. Informality is an important part of the self-help network.

During the past decade a trend in informality has entered the field of psychotherapy. Generally speaking, it is not considered unethical nor is it uncommon for a patient to know minute details of his/her therapist's life or to conduct sessions over coffee in the therapist's kitchen. Not infrequently, therapist and patient have more than a therapeutic relationship with each other. They may knowingly share the same dentist, or see each other at church or be employees in the same hospital. Blatant personal and sexual relationships between therapist and patient are considered unethical by all mental health professions, yet these sorts of relationships seem to be plentiful. I have talked with many ACOAs who were friends with a previous therapist and some who confide having had sexual contact with a therapist.

Informality in psychotherapy, studied recently by Langs, describes both the positive and negative aspects of therapeutic alliances of this nature.[13] On a positive note, informality appears to markedly increase self-esteem in the patient. Langs' interviewees reported that the "humanness" of the therapist (e.g., knowing the therapist's personal struggles, seeing the therapist in real life situations at work, etc.) was an element in the patient's experiencing the therapy as successful. The disadvantage of informality, is that major difficulties in the life of the patient, which inspired treatment in the first place, remain unchanged. This observation parallels my own experience, in that many ACOAs who report feeling wonderful about themselves following cathartic involvement in informal therapy, emerge with continued, entrenched, troubling problems.

In the years I have spent working with ACOAs in psychotherapy,

I have become increasingly convinced that to help them change behaviors which are unconsciously motivated, a formal, more traditional psychodynamic approach is most helpful. As I hope I have made clear, I favor informal peer support for substantial repair of self-esteem and altering faulty personal responsibility concepts. Since peer support is both readily available and free, I cannot justify providing informal "therapy" (which is, in fact, peer support) when the ACOA can receive this service for no charge elsewhere.

Formal psychotherapy has been well described by Langs[14] as "the ideal frame." This frame, or contract, is determined, Langs is quick to point out, by what the patient asks for, not what is expedient for the therapist. Critics of Langs attack his insistence on the use of a couch, his contention that group psychotherapy is by definition an invasion of privacy, and his steadfast belief that any third parties (including insurance carriers) seriously contaminate the treatment.[15] Bearing in mind that Langs is proposing the *ideal* contract, I do agree with several of his requirements:

- a fixed fee, a stable setting, specific and unchanging frequency of sessions, and a definite length of time.
- therapist's almost exclusive use of neutral interventions: silence, interpretation and reconstruction and management of the ground rules.
- confidentiality.
- anonymity of the therapist; personal information is deliberately withheld.[16]

In addition to these features of a desirable therapeutic contract with ACOAs, I have added two more.

A *"here and now" focus*. Unconscious aspects of behavior are most effectively demonstrated to the patient when examples of the unconscious show up during a group or individual session. The usefulness of the here and now focus was eloquently stated by Strachey.[17]

The patient's original symptoms were drained of their cathexis, and there appeared instead an artificial neurosis to which Freud gave the name "transference neurosis". The original conflicts, which had led to the onset of the neurosis,

began to be re-enacted in relation to the analyst: Now this unexpected event is far from being the misfortune that at first
sight it might seem to be. Instead of having to deal as best we
may with conflicts of the remote past, which are concerned
with dead circumstances and mummified personalities, and
whose outcome is already determined, we find ourselves involved in an actual and immediate situation, in which we and
the patient are the principal characters and the development of
which is to some extent at least under our control.

Frequent sessions. COAs are notable for having deficits in trust.
Attempting to conduct psychotherapy, either in a group or individually, by meeting once a week has severe limitations. A seven day
gap keeps the treatment alliance at a distance so great it is nearly
impossible to move beyond a superficial connection. Interestingly,
the 12 step programs of AA, Al-Anon and ACOA encourage members to attend often. It is usual for new members to go to meetings
daily for several months. The frequency of visits seems to help
overcome the trust barrier. Several years ago when I first began
conducting ACOA groups I started with weekly sessions. In a typical session, someone would present a work or relationship problem
and other members would empathize. Seldom did the session focus
on the here and now. The change in the group format to twice a
week changed the conduction of the group considerably. With frequent contact, members began to talk about how they felt toward
each other and what was happening in the room.
    This therapy contract appears to ensure ACOA patients the safety
and security they require to address unconscious drive related material. The following clinical case illustrations are provided to demonstrate how the contract just described facilitates the ACOA's ability
to address debilitating problems of unconscious origin.

CASE 1

Agnes is a reclusive 54-year-old, divorced, recovering alcoholic
mother of three sons. At the time she entered therapy for depression
and a recent suicide attempt, she had been sober five years. Previous efforts to receive help included participation in three groups

for recovering alcoholics, assertiveness training, and short term individual therapy with several therapists of varied backgrounds. The chief complaint was Agnes' relationship with her mother who lived a mile away from Agnes' apartment. Agnes described the difficulty as being unable to say no to mother, who, since Agnes was a child, had enjoyed poor health. Father, the alcoholic, died when Agnes was 12, leaving Agnes, three siblings and a sick mother.

According to Agnes, every source of help she had tried responded to her in the same way: guidance was offered on how to set limits on mother and she was encouraged to express feelings of anger about mother's infantile, demanding behavior. She voiced anger but never followed through on the limit setting. The groups (and, reportedly, her therapists) became impatient with her. When she began to feel like she was failing therapy she would quit, become more depressed and eventually would enter treatment with another person or group.

Previous interventions were of limited value to Agnes because what was perceived to be the problem, anger at mother, disguised a more distressing unconscious problem which was Agnes' terror of her mother's death. Agnes could readily talk about hating her mother, wishing she were dead so Agnes could be "really free." Clues to Agnes' fear of being aware of her need for her mother appeared in the transference.

Two months after Agnes entered psychotherapy, I took a week's vacation. When I announced my impending absence I inquired if she had any feelings about learning I would be away. With sudden hostility she threw back her head and laughed derisively, "Good God, woman," she cackled, "I've only known you six weeks. I could not care less if you take a vacation." When I pointed out that her voice sounded angry, she denied it, became even more scornful, and hurled at me a masterpiece of denial and projection, "You act like I'm supposed to be devastated because you are taking a vacation. Well, that's just stupid." I responded by saying, "If you can be angry with me, then you don't have to be aware of feeling devastated when I'm gone." This session was the beginning of months of work with Agnes in exploring why Agnes related to me as she did with everyone else: she was either angry, feigned indifference, or withdrew. Such was her life. She was nearly a recluse. But not because she didn't need people; her fear (unconscious) was that she needed them too much.

A revealing anecdote, and a turning point in the therapy, occurred after nearly a year at Christmas time, the anniversary of her suicide attempt (aspirin overdose). Her youngest son was coming to visit for five days. She talked about being busy at work Christmas week and needing to mail her son a key along with a note asking him what he wanted to do for Christmas dinner. I made the observation that her anticipated behavior transmitted a message that she was indifferent to her son's visit. She looked astonished. "Well," she said, "I just want to give him the opportunity to be with his buddies if he wants. I mean, after all, I can't expect him to sit around 24 hours a day and hold my hand, now can I?" I said, "Perhaps that's exactly what you wish he would do." Her eyes filled with tears, "But that's like I'm a clinging baby," she sobbed.

The second year of therapy when I announced a vacation Agnes sat for a minute then said, "I know I'm feeling something, my heart just leaped." When I was ill and had to cancel two sessions in a row, Agnes opened our next session by saying, "I'm sorry you were sick because I really wanted to talk to you. I needed to be here last week. But I did okay." Change in the way Agnes related to me in treatment corresponded with other changes in her life. She was noticeably less depressed. She increased her AA attendance and became involved in a folk dance group. When her mother had a mild stroke, she wept.

The major change for Agnes through psychotherapy was her increased ability to let herself love people in varying degrees without being terrorized that if she lost them she would be like an infant: hopeless and unable to take care of herself.

CASE 2

Sam, a 38-year-old divorced man entered treatment because he was upset over continual conflict with his girlfriend. It was difficult to get an accurate picture of his distress because he presented himself in a vague manner and had a penchant for discussing any problem by saying, "Then I said and then she said, and then I said. . . ." His lack of affect bordered on frightening.

Over a period of eight months, the following details emerged. Both his parents are practising alcoholics. His three brothers are alcoholic and his sister is promiscuous. For as long as he can remember his mother was flagrantly seductive with him and his brothers. Once during treatment Sam spoke of a recent visit to his parents' house. His mother, drunk, sat on his lap in a bathrobe which was so carelessly wrapped her nudity was unquestionably apparent. Sam eventually revealed a history of perversion, specifically sado-masochistic acts with a succession of women. Samples of this behavior include voyeurism (several of his friends would gang rape his "girlfriend" in his bedroom while he watched through a crack in his closet door) and other cruel acts such as bringing a date to a family gathering where his drunken brothers would make sexually insulting remarks to her.

Perversion is eroticized hate, a wedding of sorts between the sexual and aggressive drives.[18] It is an example of what can occur when little children are exposed to frankly violent and sexual behaviors. Although Sam had no memory either of seeing his parents engaging in sexual acts or of having his parents make sexual advances toward him, one can infer from the present family behavior that it would not be unlikely if one or both of these events occurred.

The common response of young children to overhearing the love-making of parents is that intercourse is an act of violence. Yukio Mishima, the late Japanese novelist, perceived lovers after intercourse as corpses.[19] In alcoholic families, parents' intercourse may in fact be a *real* act of violence. Several ACOA patients have mentioned that they occupied the bedroom next to their parents and have vivid conscious memories of father coming home drunk and listening to the sounds of screaming, hitting and brutal lovemaking in the next room. One woman I saw in treatment slept with her mother until she was ten years old. Her drunken father frequently barged in, sexually forced himself upon mother, then left the room. In all cases I have worked with where there has been violence and sexual behavior actively occurring in the presence of children, the adult result is either denial of all sexual feelings or the reverse: the patient acts out his fantasy life. This is a frequent feature of children traumatised by primal scene material.[20]

Sam lived his sexual fantasies. What he consciously wanted was a loving relationship with a woman. What he was aware of were loving feelings toward his girlfriend. He was unaware that his behavior revealed hostility toward women. His early explanation of his sexual activities was, "it may seem kinky to you but everyone always has a good time."

I saw Sam in intensive individual psychotherapy for nearly two years, at which time he was transferred to another city by his employer. Problems of the sort Sam presents are very hard to alter, but he was highly motivated. He was in pain and he wanted to feel better. In the time we met, several insights enabled Sam to make some impressive changes. He gradually realized that the pleasure he received in his treatment of women was witnessing their humiliation. "I'm just doing to them what I feel was done to me as a kid; when I was little I was humiliated by my mother's behavior towards me." He reluctantly but increasingly spoke of his wishes to humiliate me. Usually this was expressed through presenting me in a dream in which I was belittled. The more he spoke of his hostile, demeaning fantasies toward me, the less he acted them out in his life. After a year, his degrading engagements with women he periodically picked up ceased and he started attending Al-Anon meetings. He moved out of his girlfriend's apartment telling her he considered himself too sick to be in a relationship at that time. When he moved, he asked for a referral to a therapist in the city where he would be living.

These particular cases were presented to illustrate the need for psychotherapy with ACOAs who suffer from severe impairment of their ability to regulate and control drives and affects.

CONCLUSION

ACOAs are a group of co-dependents who exhibit many emotional and behavioral problems. Damage to a child from parental alcoholism may be either mild, moderate or severe. This chapter explored characteristics of the alcoholic home and the varied responses of children reared in this environment. Three major categories of problems of ACOAs were described. These included impairment in self-esteem, failure to establish reasonable concepts of personal responsibility and difficulty in appropriately regulating

, sexual and aggressive drives. The comparative value of helping the ACOA through education, peer support and psychotherapy was discussed and illustrated through detailed clinical examples.

REFERENCES

1. La Bundy, J., "Simulating Family Bonding", Focus on Family, Vol. 8, No. 5, Sept/Oct, 1985, pp. 22.

2. La Bundy, ibid., pp. 23.

3. Wegscheider, S., Another Chance, Science and Behavior Books, Palo Alto, CA, 1982.

4. Black, C., It Will Never Happen To Me, MAT Books, Denver, CO, 1982.

5. Woititz, J., Adult Children of Alcoholics, Health Communications, Inc., Pompano Beach, FL, 1983.

6. Richards, T., "Interventions with ACOAs in the Workplace", The Almacan newsletter, September, 1985, pp. 25.

7. Seixas, J. and Morehouse, E., "Children of Alcoholics", workshop, American Orthopsychiatric Association, Boston, MA, April, 1983.

8. Fox, R., "The Effect of Alcoholism on Children", In: Proceedings of the V. International Congress on Psychotherapy, Progressive Child Psychiatry, New York: Karger, Basil, 1963, pp. 55-65.

9. Nylander, I., "Children of Alcoholic Fathers", Acta Paediatric Scan: 49; 1-34, 1960.

10. Nady, E. and Offord, D., "The Offspring of Alcoholics: A Critical Review", The American Journal of Psychiatry, 134: 4, April, 1977, pp. 359.

11. Wolin, S., "Children of Alcoholics" Workshop, The American Orthopsychiatric Association, New York, 1985.

12. La Bundy, op. cit., pp. 22.

13. Langs, R, Madness and Cure, Newconcept Press, Emerson, NJ, 1985.

14. Langs, R., ibid.

15. Langs, R., "New Techniques in Psychotherapy", Workshop, Washington, DC, November 16, 1985.

16. Langs, R., Psychotherapy: A Basic Text, Aronson, New York, 1982.

17. Strachey, J., "The Nature of the Therapeutic Action of Psychoanalysis," International Journal of Psychoanalysis, Vol. 50, 1969, pp. 277.

18. Stoller, R., Perversion, Pantheon Books, New York, 1975.

19. Arlow, J., "Pyromania and the Primal Scene: A Psychoanalytic Comment on the work of Yukio Mishima," Psychoanalytic Quarterly, Vol. XLVII: 1, 1978.

20. Fenichel, O., The Psychoanalytic Theory of Neurosis, WW Norton and Co., New York, 1945.

Altering Rigid Family Role Behaviors in Families with Adolescents

Steven E. Perkins, PhD

There are millions of school-aged children living in homes where at least one parent is an alcoholic. The parenting in these homes is the responsibility of a couple where one's parenting is impacted by his/her alcoholism and the other's parenting is impacted by the stress produced by trying to cope with the effects of drinking on home life. The preoccupation of one person with alcohol and the other with coping with the alcoholic impedes the energy and ability of the couple to develop thoughtful and consistent parenting approaches. In fact, parenting is frequently inconsistent, chaotic, and self-serving in these families, and is often abdicated to an older child.

The impact of parenting in the homes of alcoholics fosters patterns of hostility (Wilson, 1982), withdrawal (Jacobs, Favorini, Meisel & Anderson, 1978) and protection (Umana, Gross & McConville, 1981) on the part of family members. In an effort to survive emotionally among the irrationality, distortion, anger, and loneliness produced in families where alcoholism is present, family members often choose ways to respond that become repetitive and rigid. Each person develops predictable ways of responding to the alcoholic and to one another that often inhibit his/her own ability to effectively share feelings, solve problems and develop close, supportive relationships.

Gradually, family members settle rigidly into roles which help to maintain the dysfunctional nature of the family interaction and to inhibit each individual's positive growth. The interruption of these

Steven E. Perkins is Founder and Director of the Akron Family Institute and Adjunct Associate Professor of Education, University of Akron, Akron, OH.

rigid role patterns is vital to individual and family health. Children from alcoholics' homes who do not break free from the rigid role behaviors will grow to reproduce, in future friend and family relationships, interaction patterns that are similar to ones developed in their families of origin. The potential transgenerational effect of maintaining rigidly held roles in relationships points to the importance of helping children and families break rigid, dysfunctional patterns.

This article will review roles commonly developed in families with an alcoholic member and discuss selected interventions that may be used to interrupt rigid, ineffective role behaviors.

FAMILY ROLES

Black (1982) and Wegscheider (1981) have identified roles that emerge in families where there is an alcoholic member. Booz, Allen & Hamilton, Inc. (1974) identified coping mechanisms which closely parallel the roles listed by Black and Wegscheider.

Wegscheider identified the roles of Hero, Scapegoat, Mascot and Lost Child as common roles in families with an alcoholic member. The Hero does what is right and is successful with grades, friends and activities. The Hero provides self-esteem for the family. He/she cannot tolerate failure and so must strive hard for success. He/she struggles with feelings of inadequacy. The Scapegoat seeks negative attention. He/she acts out and takes the focus off the alcoholic. Feelings of hurt, anger and guilt are typical for a child in this role. The Mascot helps to relieve family tension by being humorous, fun and cute. He/she is often the youngest, most immature and most protected. He/she can sense the tension and feels fearful and insecure. The Lost Child withdraws from the family, spends a lot of time alone and does not "rock the boat." He/she feels lonely, unlovable and unimportant.

Black suggested that children in homes with an alcoholic may adopt roles of Adjuster, Placater or Responsible One. The Adjuster adapts to every situation without complaint. He/she is often isolated and alone, and feels unlovable, unimportant and lonely. The Placater strives to make others feel good and ignores his/her own feelings. This person is emotionally sensitive and quickly identifies who needs to "feel better." He/she is often fearful and lonely. The Responsible One is generally compliant and assumes responsibility for providing structure and order in his or her family and life. He/she is often parenting. His/her sense of self-esteem often rests on being in control of the situation. He/she feels.lonely and is over-serious. When he/she cannot hold things together, he/she feels in-adequate.

Booz, Allen & Hamilton, Inc. (1974) have identified four coping mechanisms that children rigidly adhere to in families where there is an alcoholic: Flight, Fight, Perfect Child, and Super-Coper. The child who adopts a Flight pattern avoids being home with the alco-holic, stays in his/her room, stays emotionally distant and avoids conflict. A child who develops a Fight pattern is often aggressive and rebellious. He/she seeks negative attention. The Perfect Child does everything right. He/she is obedient and performs so that his/her parents will be proud. The Super-Coper assumes a lot of respon-sibility in the family. He/she is often parentified and can be a spousal child in the sense that he/she is an important source of emo-tional support for the co-dependent parent, perhaps becoming the "pillar" of the family.

Table 1 illustrates how the above roles seem to be similar to one another.

As these roles become more rigidly adhered to, patterns of hostil-ity, withdrawal, and protection are more strongly supported, and it becomes more injurious to the family and the individuals in it. It can be helpful to intervene in ways that help decrease the rigidity of these roles, increase the flexibility of a child to try new role behav-iors, increase the amount of sharing of feelings and decrease defen-sive behavior.

CHANGING FAMILY ROLES

Treating the family with an alcoholic member is a complex pro-cess. The following suggestions are tools that may be helpful in facilitating change. Each intervention must be considered against the total treatment plan to evaluate its potential usefulness in help-ing to alter family role behavior.

Table 1

Coping Roles

Authors	Coping Roles			
Black	Adjuster		Placater	Responsible One
Booz, Allen and Hamilton	Flight	Fight	Perfect Child	Super-Coper Perfect Child
Wegscheider	Lost Child	Scapegoat	Mascot	Family Hero

Sculpting

Sculpting is a technique that involves using spatial relations to symbolize the nature of the emotional relationships in the family (Papp, 1976). It can be used with a family, adolescent group or multi-family group to educate about family roles and develop increased awareness of one's position in his/her family.

First, the counselor identifies the common roles found in the alcoholic family and discusses the accompanying feelings and behaviors associated with these roles.

Second, persons are chosen to depict a "typical" family with an alcoholic member. The counselor then directs the sculpting. For example, the father in the family is alcoholic. The counselor places him in the middle of the room, standing on a chair. The mother is placed in front of him, facing away and smiling. The child who has the Hero role is placed in close proximity to mother, whose hand is outstretched to him/her. The Lost Child is placed in a distant corner of the room and may be reading or listening to music. He/she is turned away from the other family members. The Scapegoat is placed near the door with his/her back to the family, while Mother and Father point accusing fingers at him/her. The Mascot is asked to run around the room distracting playfully.

Up to this point, participants in the sculpting have been instructed to participate without verbal interaction. Now the counselor can direct the "family members" to discuss what each role feels like. If other people are present, the audience can participate in the discussion. The feelings, behaviors and purposes of each role can be addressed as the dialogue continues.

Third, an adolescent can be chosen to sculpt his/her family as he/she sees the roles and relationships that are present. Further dialogue helps to process feelings and ideas that can assist those present to integrate the information that has been presented. In an adolescent group, it is helpful to have each person take turns constructing his/her family, using the group members to sculpt the relationships as he/she perceives them.

Journal

Frequently, adolescents are unclear or unaware of their feelings and behaviors and how their reactions are connected to other family members. Keeping a journal can help an adolescent to untangle the confusion. Clear and specific instructions are necessary to maximize the effect of this task. Daily, the adolescent should identify:

1. Feelings experienced during the day.
2. The situation that surrounded each feeling, such as who was present, where it took place, what was said, and how people behaved.

For those who have difficulty identifying feelings, a feelings checklist can be used to help stimulate appropriate identification. Also, the order of entry into the journal could be changed to identify:

1. Situations where there was interaction with others.
2. The feelings that accompanied that interaction.

Through writing in the journal and discussing the entries in a group or in the family, the adolescent can explore the effects of his/ her feelings and behaviors on himself/herself and others. Careful guidance by the counselor can lead the adolescent to enhanced insight and understanding of repetitive and rigid patterns that he/she participates in. Where interaction has not been productive to harmonious relationships, the stage is set to consider new ways of interacting.

Sequencing

Another intervention designed to increase awareness and set the stage for interrupting rigid role patterns is sequencing. This involves asking a series of questions that helps to clarify the sequence of feelings and behaviors involved in conflictual and often hurtful experiences in the family. To do this:

1. Identify the behaviors of each family member that are most likely to generate an angry or hurt reaction from others. Questions like these may be used: "Jim, what does Dad do that leads you to feel hurt and/or angry?" or "Dad, what can Jim do that will set you off?"

2. Track the string of behaviors that are exchanged after the conflictual sequence begins. For example, if Jim says that Dad ignores him when he talks, the counselor can begin with the ignoring behavior and uncover the sequence that follows: Dad ignores Jim — Jim feels hurt and makes a sarcastic remark — Dad feels angry and scolds Jim — Jim feels hurt and angry and berates Dad for being uninterested — Dad tells Jim that he's grounded — Jim slams the door and leaves the house or withdraws to his room.

3. Asking what others do while Dad and Jim are in conflict helps to clarify how the entire family adapts to this situation.

Through sequencing, the major rigid and repetitive conflictual patterns can be identified, and the counselor will have a clear map for determining appropriate places for intervention in order to interrupt the patterns.

Trading or Changing Roles

Interrupting rigidity of roles requires persistence and carefully planned strategies. Trading roles can help. When used in the family, the counselor must identify the roles each person plays and the major repetitive sequences in which the family becomes involved. Two persons are then assigned to roles and two others are assigned as their coaches, to make sure that they act out the roles accurately. The major sequences are rehearsed in the session, having each person behave in the new role. Where it is not possible to have two coaches, the counselor can act as a coach.

In an adolescent group, the person is assigned a new role and a coach, with other group members playing the family. The major family sequences are rehearsed in the session. The adolescent is then assigned to practice the new role in his/her family and to report how it affected family interaction.

The awareness gained by trading or changing roles can break the automatic response pattern that was in place. This increases the possibility that more constructive interactions can be introduced.

Negotiating Alternatives

Once the roles and the patterns surrounding them are clear, the possibility of negotiating for changes is increased. Negotiating for different interaction from others in order to step out of rigid roles can be facilitated with the following process:

1. Through sequencing, identify interactional patterns that are destructive to the family relationship and significant in maintaining the rigid roles.
2. Choose one sequence and identify the person who initiates it.
3. Have the initiator identify what the other person could do that would help him/her behave in a different way to circumvent the conflictual pattern.
4. The second person who behaves in the sequence can agree to behave as requested, or offer an alternative that could serve the same purpose, but would be more to his/her liking.
5. If person #2 agrees, then it is his/her turn to ask for a behavior

that would help him/her behave more constructively to alter the rigid role behavior. If person #2 offers an alternative, then person #1 can accept the alternative or suggest another option. The exchange continues until both agree on an alternative that person #2 can do to interrupt the rigid patterns of interaction.

6. Each person takes turns identifying and negotiating for changes the other can make until each person has at least four alternatives they can try out to help interrupt a sequence that has been defined as destructive to the relationships in the family and as significant in maintaining rigid role behavior.

When each person has alternatives that have been collaboratively determined, then a series of role plays can be implemented to practice the identified sequence, using different combinations of the alternative behaviors. The counselor can participate in the role plays and model the alternatives, can be a reactive member, making the other work hard to implement alternatives, or can coach family members as they practice new behavior.

Negotiating for changes in interaction and practicing to increase the chance for success is hard work, but can leave positive results (Azrin, Naster & Jones, 1973).

Enactment

Enactment is the process of recreating a situation that occurred between sessions by having family members carry out their roles in the event in front of the counselor (Minuchin & Fishman, 1981). First, the replay offers the family an opportunity to view themselves in a less charged atmosphere. Second, the counselor can intervene and ask family members to behave differently to see if it feels better. An effective "coach" can capitalize on the family's specific experience to initiate and practice more helpful alternatives.

Writing Letters

Just as the journal can help adolescents begin to sort out thoughts and feelings, writing letters to family members can help organize feelings and thoughts that need to be communicated. If possible, the letters should include:

1. Any positive feelings and thoughts that the adolescent experiences.
2. The hurts they have experienced and how the other person could help them get over the hurt.
3. The desire for healing.
4. The commitment to do their part to help make things change.

The counselor must coach the adolescent in his/her writing until the letter is sufficiently clear, honest, and constructive and the adolescent is ready to read it to the appropriate family member. Utilizing letters can help family members organize and share information in a way that minimizes threat and maximizes listening.

CONCLUSION

Rigid family roles, if left unchanged, are carried by adolescents from their family of origin into other work, friend, and family relationships. Dysfunctional patterns are transferred across generations, affecting many lives.

Interrupting rigid role patterns in families is a challenging process involving the need to increase knowledge and awareness and to help members generate alternative patterns that can be integrated into the family interaction. This paper discussed some of the tools that can be used to facilitate the process of change. The ability of the counselor to effectively integrate these into the overall treatment process will determine their usefulness in increasing role flexibility and interrupting rigid role interaction.

REFERENCES

Azrin, N., Naster, B., & Jones, R. (1973). Reciprocity counseling: A rapid learning based procedure for marital counseling. *Behavior Research and Therapy, 11*, 365-382.
Black, C. (1982). *It Will Never Happen To Me*. Denver: M.A.C.
Booz, Allen & Hamilton, Inc. (1974). An assessment of needs and resources for children of alcoholic parents. National Institute of Alcohol Abuse and Alcoholism.
Jacob, T., Favorini, A., Meisel, A., & Anderson, C. (1978). The alcoholic

spouse, children and family interactions: Substantive findings and method-ological issues. *Journal of Studies on Alcohol, 39*, 1231-1251.

Minuchin, S. & Fishman, C. (1981). *Family Therapy Techniques*. Cambridge: Howard University Press.

Papp, P. (1976). Family Choreography. In P. J. Guerin, Jr. (Ed.), *Family Therapy: Theory and Practice*. New York: Gardner Press.

Umana, R., Gross, S., & McConville, M. (1981). *Crisis In The Family: Three Approaches*. New York: Gardner Press.

Wegscheider, S. (1981). *Another Chance*. Palo Alto: Science and Behavior Books, Inc.

Wilson, C. (1982). The impact on children. In J. Orford and J. Harwin (Eds.), *Alcohol and the Family*. New York: St. Martin's Press.

The Lonely Journey:
Lesbians and Gay Men
Who Are Co-dependent

Dana G. Finnegan, PhD, CAC
Emily B. McNally, MEd, CAC

SUMMARY. Co-dependence can be defined as a disorder of the relationship of the self to the self and to others. The denial of self in order to feel connected to others is at the heart of co-dependence. People create a false self in order to be who they think others want them to be because they cannot tolerate the fear of being alone or abandoned. Schaef and Cermak both state that this denial of true self is the hallmark of co-dependence, and Schaef contends that society's institutions teach co-dependence. Society's homophobic teachings merge with and intensify its teachings about co-dependence and make gay/lesbian people and those with sexual identity issues especially vulnerable to becoming co-dependent. The implications for treatment for gay/lesbian co-dependents are particularly that skilled counselors need to be knowledgeable about issues and problems specific to lesbians and gay men and take a creative approach to working with a non-traditional population.

Much has been written in the past few years about co-dependence—what it is and is not, what causes it, how to treat it. Very little has been written about co-dependence as it relates to and affects lesbians and gay men. This article is an attempt to address this lack in the literature.

In her book *Co-Dependence: Misunderstood-Mistreated*, Ann Wilson Schaef contends that co-dependence must be viewed within the context of *all* the primary systems: the personal system of the individual, the family, the institutions, and society at large. It must

Dana G. Finnegan and Emily B. McNally are affiliated with the National Association of Lesbian and Gay Alcoholism Professionals, New York, NY.

121

be seen within this context because the culture *trains* people to be co-dependent. This way of viewing the development and the playing out of co-dependence is both appropriate and helpful for examining the sources and extra power of co-dependence in gay men and lesbians because so many of their attitudes and behaviors are oppressively shaped by the homophobia in their families, their institutions, and their society.

Using Schaef's definitions and characteristics of co-dependence and Timmen Cermak's observations as the basis for discussion, this article will focus on three matters: (1) the ways that society's homophobic teachings merge with and intensify its teachings about co-dependence when the "pupils" are struggling with possibilities of being homosexual or are aware of being gay or lesbian; (2) the ways these homophobic teachings make gay/lesbian people and those with sexual identity issues especially vulnerable to co-dependence; and (3) the implications of these factors for treatment.

This culture teaches everyone to be homophobic. The messages are loud and clear — gay men and lesbians are sick, immoral, unnatural. They are disgusting; they are to be despised. But since homosexuals do in fact exist, then the only remedy is for them to *be invisible*. As long as they're silent, stay in the closet, and don't make themselves noticeable, society will grudgingly tolerate their existence. If, out of fear and self-hatred, gay men and lesbians follow society's dictates that they not come out, they must create a *false self*. They cannot reveal who they really are; they cannot freely and openly act upon their true feelings. They must constantly lie about self, both overtly and covertly. They must learn to "pass" as heterosexual in order to survive. In effect, society says to them: "Your true identity is not valid; you must put society's wants, feelings, and beliefs before yours — no matter what the price; you must meet society's expectations, for only by doing so will you gain any meaning." It is no wonder, then, that lesbians and gay men learn that "I am who I think you want me to be." It is this construction of a false self which, we contend, lies at the heart of *all* co-dependence. People who grow up with sexual identities different from those of the mainstream receive a double dose of co-dependence teachings.

Drawing on this description, we will discuss how growing up and living in a homophobic society prepares people who may be or who are gay or lesbian to be co-dependent as defined and described by Schaef. Primarily, we will focus on how being gay or lesbian gives extra force to their co-dependence.

Schaef contends that via the institutions of the family, the schools, and the church, society *trains* people in the ways of co-dependence. For example, she notes society's approval of the love-sick, romantic entanglement which is called love and which is promoted as the way to live in a marriage. Yet what this really does is foster unhealthy dependence or what she calls relationship addiction.

CHARACTERISTICS OF CO-DEPENDENCE

Schaef presents and discusses a number of characteristics of the disease of co-dependence. The primary characteristic is that of "external referenting," i.e., receiving one's meaning from outside oneself. This need to gain meaning from external sources results from having little or no sense of self or sense of inner meaning. This condition lies at the heart of co-dependence and is created and powered by an incredibly strong fear of being alone or abandoned. As Cermak notes, this fear "is so great that violence against one's own needs is tolerated" (p. 17). He goes on to point out that, "When the line is crossed into co-dependence, that sense of [true] self is compromised and even lost" (p. 13).

People who have little if any sense of their intrinsic meaning, who have little sense of self, tend to be addicted to relationships no matter how bad because relationships provide meaning and at least create the illusion of protection against feelings of aloneness and abandonment. Such relationships are characterized by intense dependency on the part of each person and by a great lack of boundaries between them.

Lack of Boundaries

Schaef explains that since they lack boundaries, co-dependents tend to take on another's feelings and thoughts. She contends that family, school, and church teach people to do so. As she says,

This is *cultural co-dependence* [our italics]. We learn that the reference point for thinking, feeling, seeing, and knowing is external to the self, and this training produces people without boundaries. (p. 46)

Cermak agrees that distorted boundaries are a major issue in co-dependence: "The co-dependent equates closeness with compliance and intimacy with fusion" (p. 18).

The relationship between these characteristics of co-dependence and the realities of being gay or lesbian is powerful and profound. By definition, "homosexual" means being sexually attracted to person(s) of the same sex. By extension, homosexual, or preferably gay/lesbian means being sexually and often affectionally attracted to persons of the same sex and *therefore* persons with the same gender socialization. In essence, gay people are attracted to and relate to other people who are socialized in the same ways. The other person in the relationship has received the same teachings about ways of "being in the world" and about ways of seeing self. Such similarities between people's socialization can have a profound effect on the ways they see one another, especially when they get into relationships. The lack of sharp distinctions based on gender role teachings strongly increases the potential for two people of the same sex to see one another as extensions of self. Thus the boundaries between self and other are oftentimes not clear, a condition which supports, contributes to, and intensifies co-dependence.

Another aspect of this phenomenon can also come into play. Peter Nardi discusses the differences between "the nature of intimate, dyadic relationships" of gays and lesbians and heterosexuals. He contends that "The most important [difference] is the absence of traditionally defined roles based on gender" (p. 86). Nardi notes how this absence creates a potential for power and equality conflicts and allows for the construction of one's own rules and roles. While these conditions may provide possibilities for freer, more creative relationships, they also provide strong possibilities of fusion resulting from unclear or nonexistent boundaries. Of course, if one or both of the members of the relationship is the adult child of alcoholism, the whole issue of boundaries is further confounded.

Denial of Self

Lack of boundaries and confusion of identities between self and others are inextricably linked to what Cermak considers the central feature of co-dependence: "Denial of the self *for the sake of feeling connected to others* [our italics] is the hallmark of co-dependence. It creates a profound void within the self" (pp. 17-18). Cermak further comments that because people so fear abandonment they create a *false self*—in order to have and maintain the relationship, in order to feel connected to others.

Being gay or lesbian (or even having questions about one's sexual identity) is perfect training for co-dependence. In most places, times, and circumstances in America, it is emotionally, socially, financially, and often physically dangerous to reveal one's gayness. The culture's homophobic dictates make that clear. So if people are or think they might be gay or lesbian, they *know* not to reveal who they really are. Young people learn very early to create a "false self"—a "heterosexual self" which is acceptable to others, which can be safely presented to others. They learn how to "pass" as heterosexual; they learn to hide, to bury, their true self and reveal it only in the most selective ways and circumstances. Often, young people will create this fraudulent heterosexual self in order to "belong" and take part in the heterosexual dating scene during their teenage and early adult years. They learn not to talk about their real feelings, interests, relationships in the workplace—or any other place. *In order to feel connected to others*—whether family, society, friends, church, teachers—the gay or lesbian person will deny the true self and create a false self presentable to these others.

For many people who are or fear they may be gay, the price of "coming out," of revealing the true self is intolerably high. But the price of creating and maintaining a false self, of passing, is alienation, isolation, great anxiety, depression, abandonment of self—an unbearably high price also. As long as homophobia (both from outside the person and from within) poisons the atmosphere, the dilemma is close to insoluble, and the stress is incredible.

On a daily basis, the gay/lesbian person who passes as "straight" lives with the anxiety (no matter how subtle) of being discovered, unmasked, found out. The constant, underlying message is, "What if they knew who I *really* am? What if they found out?'' This belief that only the false self is acceptable, that the true self is not acceptable is the core of co-dependent thinking. "Who I truly am is no good; therefore, in order for me to gain your acceptance, I will deny *me* and be who I think you want me to be." Society demands that gays be invisible *as gays* in order to be connected to (accepted by) society. This means that gay people learn to *appear* or *seem* to be not gay to gain the connection. That is the ultimate in *external referenting* — tell me who I should appear to be and I will be it. What better training in co-dependence can one get?

Control Issues

Although control most certainly is central to all aspects of co-dependence, it is helpful to separate it out here in order to examine how it operates in particular contexts.

Impression Management

Schaef calls certain forms of control Impression Management — co-dependents attempt to control how others will see and feel about them because "they truly believe that if they can just become [or be] what others want, they will be safe and accepted" (p. 48). It is this same belief that keeps the gay or lesbian person's closet door locked. Schaef further points out that,

> Co-dependents are totally dependent on others for their very right to exist. If they are not validated and approved from the outside, they think they do not even have a right to be on this planet. (p. 49)

This drive to be validated and approved is tremendously strong for gays who feel so *in*validated and so *dis*approved by society's and their own internalized homophobic standards. But gays are caught in a cruel paradox: who they truly are cannot be known and available for validation unless they are "out of the closet" as gay, i.e., unless their true self is disclosed. Yet if they disclose as gay, society's homophobia negates, invalidates, and violently disapproves of them. Paradoxically, if they show society their false self, i.e., pass as heterosexual, then the validation and approval will be granted to the person they only seem to be, not to the person they really are. The loss of self and the sense of invisible *non-being* are profound and form the bedrock of co-dependence.

Impression management becomes a vital skill for gays who want or need to be closeted. It becomes the way they can exist in a hostile environment. And probably because many lesbians and gay men become very adept at managing others' impressions or perceptions of them, i.e., passing successfully, they create for themselves an illusion of control. For while they can, in fact, control much of the information that shapes others' perceptions of them, they cannot control others' knowledge of them *as they truly are*. It is a hollow victory, indeed, to control others' vision only by distorting that vision.

Controlling Self and Others

Cermak discusses co-dependents' "distorted relationship to willpower," their belief that they can control their own and significant other people's lives by "sheer force of will" (p. 12). Hand in hand with this belief is another that the co-dependent is responsible for whatever happens to and is done by the significant others. There is a confusion of identities, a breakdown of boundaries between the co-dependent and the significant other(s). The co-dependent's sense of self becomes obscured or lost and his or her "self-worth rises or falls with his or her partner's success or failure" (p. 12). When confusion of identities unites with a distorted idea of willpower, the result is that

> In order for the co-dependent to feel good, his or her partner must be happy and behave in appropriate ways. If the partner is not happy, the co-dependent feels responsible for *making* him or her happy. (p. 13)

Two particular aspects of gay/lesbian experience are especially pertinent to these phenomena of co-dependence. As most lesbians and gay men grow up in this culture, they receive repeated messages that they must "protect" others from the truth of their identity. And most gay men and lesbians learn very well how to shield their family, their friends, their schoolmates, their teachers, indeed most people from the truth. It is not uncommon to hear gay men and lesbians fervently state that "It would *kill* my parents if they knew I was gay." Other gay people can relate experiences of rejection by family or friends when they came out to these significant others. It is almost inevitable that gays would learn that they are somehow *responsible* for others' feelings, that they must control others' perceptions. Such are the beliefs that co-dependence is made of.

The other important aspect of gay/lesbian experience is that of gay male and lesbian couples when remaining closeted is an issue. If, as is usually the case, the gays involved in couples have some internalized homophobia, then one or both are likely to want to remain closeted. But if one is more homophobic than the other, then the more homophobic one probably will try to control the other's appearance and behavior. The more homophobic partner is likely to send such messages as, "Don't act so effeminate/masculine"; "Don't look at me so openly"; "Don't use words like 'gay' out loud." The more homophobic partner's self-esteem is strongly tied to the other partner's appearance and behavior. The pressure to not stand out in a crowd, to be "invisible," is very powerful. Perfect training for co-dependence.

Feelings

Schaef discusses the characteristic of being out of touch with feelings. As she says,

> Co-dependents have become so preoccupied in fulfilling others' expectations that they have lost touch with themselves. They are so trained . . . to see others' points of view that they always put those viewpoints above their own. Co-dependents believe that when they *understand* how another feels, they have no right to have feelings of their own. *In order to be accepted, they deny their own experience.* (pp. 57-58)

Being lesbian or gay in this homophobic culture trains people to be supersensitive to and to put others' wants and needs and feelings and viewpoints above their own. Gay people learn well and early the central message that *to be accepted* they must in fact deny their own experience, their own true, inner self. These teachings have an extremely powerful effect, educating them in the ways of victim-hood. What Cermak says of co-dependents applies to gays also: "the fear of being alone or abandoned [or rejected] . . . is so great that violence against one's own needs is tolerated" (p. 17).

Physical Illnesses

Both Schaef and Cermak cite stress-related physical illnesses as a characteristic of co-dependence. These include such illnesses as headaches; gastrointestinal problems; rheumatoid arthritis; hyper-tension; peptic ulcer. In addition, co-dependents are prone to chem-ical dependency and/or other addictions. Cermak contends that *"substance abuse is consistent with the personality structure of the co-dependent"* (p. 29). Schaef comments that she believes co-de-pendents frequently "become ill *from attempting to control the un-controllable* [our italics]" (p. 54).

Although there is no research yet to link various stress-related illnesses (other than alcoholism) to the problems of dealing with homophobia, there is no question that being oppressed by a ho-mophobic society is indeed stressful. It also seems quite clear that being lesbian or gay in this culture teaches gay people all the les-sons of co-dependence.

Two relevant factors need to be noted here. Although some of the research on the incidence of alcohol abuse and alcoholism among gay men and lesbians is flawed, all of the studies show a remarkable consistency in their findings. These are that 28 to 32 percent of lesbians and gay men are at high risk or are alcoholic. The other factor is that there are strong indications that susceptibility to AIDS and ARC is stress-related.

THE CULTURAL CONTEXT OF CO-DEPENDENCE

After discussing the characteristics of co-dependence, Schaef ex-amines in some detail the role of societal institutions in teaching people to be co-dependent. She looks at how the family, the schools, and the church train people in this culture to "freeze" feelings; be perfectionistic and therefore be set up to fail and feel inadequate; to be dishonest about feelings that are not "socially acceptable''; and to think in confused, obsessive ways. This training, she contends, helps create co-dependents.

Throughout this article, we have described the homophobic teachings of this society which are conveyed to gay men and lesbians by these same institutions — the family, the schools, the church. All of them teach lesbians and gay men to freeze or deny their sexual/affectional feelings and to hide their feelings as unacceptable. They teach that if people are gay or lesbian they *cannot* measure up, that they are inferior when measured against the heterosexual ideal. They teach that the true self of the gay person is not socially acceptable and is to be kept hidden. And it teaches gays to think in confused and obsessive ways about themselves and their fitness as members of the culture.

The parallels are harrowing. The effects are devastating.

IMPLICATIONS FOR TREATMENT

Cermak contends that "co-dependence exists on a par with other personality disorders — such as borderline" and needs, therefore, to be treated with "the depth of psychodynamic psychotherapy required to treat characterological issues" (pp. 61-62). Treating co-dependents requires that the therapist have a knowledge of psychodynamics and character disorders and be experienced in using psychotherapeutic techniques. In addition, of course, the therapist must be thoroughly versed in both co-dependence and chemical dependence and in addictionology, also.

Treating co-dependents who are lesbians or gay men requires all of the above plus some further qualifications. Therapists need to have worked through their own homophobia and to be clear that being gay or lesbian is well within the parameters of health. If therapists believe that being gay or lesbian is somehow inferior or less healthy, then they will add to the gay/lesbian co-dependent's burden of self-doubt, low self-esteem, and feelings of invalidation.

Therapists also need to have a clear understanding of the parallels and links between co-dependence and gays' responses to homophobia — as discussed in this article. Therapists need to have a thorough grasp of what the stages of recovery from co-dependence entail and what the stages of *recovery from homophobia* entail and how those two similar processes interface with each other. (For a discussion of the co-dependent's recovery process, see Cermak. For a discussion of the stages of developing a positive gay male or lesbian identity, see Finnegan and McNally's book.)

Therapists need to be especially attentive to issues specific to gay men and lesbians.

- Therapists need to routinely ask all clients what their sexual orientation is so that the therapists can attend to the special issues of those who are gay or lesbian or who may be unclear about their sexual identity.
- In order to find and help gay and lesbian co-dependents who are the Significant Others (SO) of chemically dependent clients, it is important to think creatively. For example, the members of gay or lesbian couples may not live together and in fact may live some distance from one another. A gay or lesbian person's "family" may well consist of close friends (Nardi, 1982). Or the SO may be a gay or lesbian parent or child.
- Many gays have strong feelings of alienation in reaction to the homophobia of the larger culture and the "alcophobia" of the gay/lesbian subcultures. Thus a gay male or lesbian couple may have an intense feeling that their relationship is a proposition of "You and me against the world," which constitutes a crazy glue not easily undone. Or the non-chemically dependent partner may be very worried that sobriety will ruin their social life because drinking/drugging constitutes such a powerful norm in the gay/lesbian subcultures. Therapists need to assist their clients in developing social support networks which are less alcohol and drug oriented and in recognizing that sober socializing is possible—even fun.
- Therapists need to help gay/lesbian co-dependents work through their internalized homophobia because it feeds co-dependence. In addition, therapists need to serve as reality touchstones regarding external homophobia—to reassure clients that this culture is indeed homophobic and that the client is not crazy. In effect, by helping clients see the difference between their own characterological issues and those of soci-

ety, therapists can help clients draw strong and healthy boundaries between them and an often cruel and rejecting society and learn to distinguish between supportive and non-supportive folk. Therapists can also help clients realize that being lesbian or gay can be a positive life experience.

- In discussing the importance of referring clients to self-help groups such as Alanon, Cermak states that *"There is really no time in therapy when such referrals are inappropriate"* (p. 67). For therapists working with gay/lesbian co-dependents, it is imperative to keep in mind that referring to some groups may be inappropriate because they are not safe places for gays to self-disclose. Many lesbians and gay men report having to change the pronoun when discussing their SO because of the group's homophobia. Therapists must know which Alanon and ACOA groups are *safe* for lesbians and gay men.
- Safety is a critical issue. If a co-dependent partner is deeply closeted (e.g., in order not to risk being fired), then insisting that he or she attend a family program may drive this person away from treatment. Therapists may need to honor gay people's very real and realistic fears of disclosure and work individually or with the couple even though a group experience would ordinarily be the preferred mode of treatment.
- Above all else, confidentiality must be protected and assured. Gay men and lesbians have been hurt too many times by the disclosure of their sexual orientation. Gay parents have lost custody of their children; gay men and lesbians have been fired, have lost their apartments, have been disowned by family and rejected by friends. Therapists must be aware of these very real dangers for their lesbian and gay male clients and should honor the need for stringent protections of confidentiality.

In order to do their work knowledgeably and effectively, therapists must have a good knowledge of the special resources available for gay men and lesbians. In addition, it is most helpful for therapists to develop a network of lesbians and gays who can help support gay/lesbian clients as they struggle to recover. In particular, therapists can avail themselves of the major resource offered by the

National Association of Lesbian and Gay Alcoholism Professionals (see References).

CONCLUSION

This article is an initial theoretical look at co-dependence as it interfaces with lesbians and gay men's responses to homophobia. This approach is intended to help establish a new perspective on gay/lesbian co-dependents. It is merely a beginning, but hopefully a beginning of seeing gay/lesbian co-dependents distinct from their chemically dependent other but in the context of homophobic oppression. Hopefully, too, others will take these ideas and build on them.

Perhaps the most important concept considered in this article and the one most salient to good treatment is that homophobia teaches all the characteristics of co-dependence. As Hackney (1985) says, "co-dependency can be approached as basically a disorder of the relationship with the self by an individual who feels invisible or overlooked . . ." (p. 5). If a person is lesbian or gay (or even unsure about sexual identity) and heeds the homophobic dictates of society, she or he will learn to split the self off into true and false self. This creation of a false self lies at the heart of being closeted and of being co-dependent. Knowledge of this concept and its effects must inform and guide therapists' treatment of their lesbian and gay male co-dependent clients if that treatment is to be truly effective.

REFERENCES

Cermak, T. L. (1986). *Diagnosing and Treating Co-Dependence.* Minneapolis: Johnson Institute.

Finnegan, D. G., & McNally, E. B. (1987). *Dual Identities: Counseling Chemically Dependent Gay Men and Lesbians.* Center City, MN: Hazelden.

Hackney, E. (1986). Gay/Lesbian Co-Dependency and Self-Oppression. Paper presented at the Seventh National Lesbian/Gay Health Conference, March, 1986, Washington, DC.

Nardi, P. (1982). Alcohol Treatment and the Non-Traditional "Family" Structures of Gays and Lesbians. *Journal of Alcohol and Drug Education, 27*(2), 83-89.

National Association of Lesbian and Gay Alcoholism Professionals (NALGAP). National headquarters: 1208 East State Blvd., Fort Wayne, IN 46805; (219)

483-8280; Clearinghouse: 204 West 20th St., New York, NY 10011; (212) 807-0634.

Schaef, A. W. (1986). *Co-Dependence: Misunderstood, Mistreated*. Minneapolis: Winston Press.

Whitney, S. (1982). The Ties That Bind: Strategies for Counseling the Gay Male Co-Alcoholic, *Journal of Homosexuality*, 7(4), 37-43.

The Recovering Couples Group: A Viable Treatment Alternative

Paul Shields, EdD

There is a strong likelihood that the clinician working with recovering couples will be greatly influenced by general systems theory (Bertalanfly, 1968) and the family therapy movement. The basic premise of general systems theory approach is that each person in the family, as a part of the family unit, contributes to the overall level of family functioning with regard to symptom development. The interaction among family members is thus a critical determinant in the formation of family dynamics. Alcoholism is an integral component of family functioning and each person tends to fulfill certain predictable roles within the family system (Wegscheider, 1981; McCrady, 1982). The problem of alcoholism is not merely consequential to the drinking but more critically the system functioning that completes the psychodynamics of the family system (Steinglass, Weiner and Mendelson, 1971; Berenson, 1976). Alcoholism from the systems perspective is therefore purposeful, adaptive, and homeostatic.

PREVIOUS RESEARCH ON RECOVERING COUPLES GROUPS

Presently, alcoholism is still ranked high by clinicians to be among the most difficult problem to treat (Geiss and O'Leary, 1981), and little information is revealed in the literature on alcohol-complicated marriages (Paolino and McCrady, 1977; Geiss and O'Leary, 1981). Burton and Kaplan (1968) evaluated couples in treatment, hypothesizing that family dysfunction and excessive drinking were mutually reinforcing and that which symptom pre-

135

ceded which was irrelevant to treatment. Of those couples fol-
lowed-up, the data suggested that a majority reported fewer marital
problems (75%); 47.4% denied any negative consequences associated with drinking; and 55.6% reported abstinence or a decrease in
drinking up to the collection of follow-up data. The study also suggested that the probability of diminished drinking episodes was influenced by fewer number of areas of strong disagreement between
spouses. Although there are limitations to their work, Burton and
Kaplan's studies represent one of the first attempts to evaluate the
importance of couples' therapy in the treatment of alcoholism
(Paolino and McCrady, 1977). The work of other researchers
(Smith, 1969; Gallant, Rich, Bly and Terranova, 1970; Paolino and
McCrady, 1976) suggest that couples' group therapy may lead to
successful treatment outcome in less than 50% of the cases treated.
Due to lack of control groups, self-report data by the spouses and
the effects of various defense mechanisms, study results are likely
to have been distorted to an unknown degree (Paolino and Mc-
Crady, 1977).

  This writer's work with recovering couples has involved an inte-
gration of the systems model and the disease concept model of treatment. Contrary to theoretical purists, I have found that a potentiated
process is effected when utilizing components from each perspective. It is from systems theory that the residual maladaptive, homeostatic behaviors can be challenged. However, intervention has
no chance for success unless a commitment to abstinence is made,
and there is no active alcoholism to contaminate the therapeutic
process. The power of the disease concept in recovery serves this
vital purpose of keeping the marital system free of alcohol so that
intervention efforts can have maximum potential for effectiveness.

SYMBIOTIC ISSUES

  The concept of symbiosis plays a central role in working with
recovering couples. As a phenomenon of adult dysfunction, symbiotic relationships are characterized by poor psychological boundaries, an overabundance of projective material, frequent use of
blame and guilt, and intense love/hate ambivalence (Beavers,
1985). The degree of differentiation (Bowen, 1971) can be consid-

ered at the lowest level of functioning in which each spouse is excessively dependent on the feelings of their partner. Most of one's personal energy is invested in maintaining conflict-free interaction, obtaining "love" or feeling comfortable. There is no differentiation between feeling and intellect. The use of the word "I" is in terms of desires or personal pain rather than convictions or beliefs (Paolino and McCrady, 1977).

FOUR CRITICAL AREAS OF RECOVERY

As the much desired reality of abstinence settles in on the couple at a preconscious level, a major disruption of roles, rules and boundary parameters occurs and emotional stress escalates rather than diminishes. Couples in the initial period of recovery are often fearful, tense, silently engaged in control struggles at a covert level, and pursuing different hidden agendas. Recovery then is simultaneously a blessing and a curse. The long-hoped-for abstinence leaves in its wake a distorted self-concept, a fear of conflict frequently with phobic proportions, confusion and repression of feelings and a general sense of increased family tension. It is around these four basic areas of functioning; self-concept, conflict resolution, identification and expression of feelings, and development of leisure skills that crucial work with recovering couples is done in a group milieu. Each area is extremely vital to basic healthy functioning and too often lacks both emphasis and awareness by the recovering couple. Frequently, the limited knowledge of these areas by recovering couples is spoken by a spouse in a calm but fragile, tone, "I would like us to learn how to communicate better." It is not difficult to sense the deep desperation of each spouse beneath this verbal request.

During the active using period, spouses evolve methods of diverting emphasis away from self-oriented issues. The chemically dependent was lost to the preoccupation of usage and the co-dependent was lost to the preoccupation of the chemically dependent and in assuming responsibilities for the chemically dependent. In recovery, each person is squarely faced with responsibility for themselves, not their spouse. Self-concept now must be redefined in terms of "me," not him or her. This adjustment affects the chemically dependent and the co-dependent in both similar and distinctively different ways.

The marital system is accustomed to functioning at interactional extremes; in total control or out of control, loving or hating, elated or depressed, emotionally distant or totally intimate. This dichotomous process is carried over into the self-concept of each spouse as each secretly determines themselves as either good or bad, in love or hating, right or wrong, guilty or blameless. Ultimately, this process sets the tone for a great deal of inner conflict that is more frequently projected onto the spouse than resolved independently of the spouse. Both the chemically dependent and the co-dependent share this symbiotic commonality.

There are also distinctive differences with regard to how self-concept is affected in recovery by each spouse. The chemically dependent can no longer depend on previous manipulations to keep the usage active. Since interpersonal skills were manipulative in nature, he is left with virtually no clear idea of how to interact in a healthy manner with his spouse. He is most fearful that he will be "found out" regarding his feelings which are experienced most intensely during this initial phase of recovery and basically perceives himself as psychologically stripped of control. Compliance/defiance, control/out of control, anger/guilt are common conflicts, all of which are projected, displaced or repressed by the chemically dependent. In essence, the recovering chemically dependent's self-concept is at best distorted and limited to how he believes himself to be perceived by significant others. Unfortunately, he often experiences more anger or other negative feelings from his spouse more prominently than when he was actively using.

The self-concept of the co-dependent during initial recovery is characterized by fear. Although sobriety is greatly desired, it brings with it a total shift in the family dynamics. The co-dependent is no longer able to use his role as "emotionally strong" or "angel of mercy" and his critical sense of importance is lost. The years of being totally responsible (which evolved into controlling, over-responsibility) and which was a strong factor in his self-identity is threatened as the chemically dependent begins attempting to take over long abandoned role expectations. Another type of fear exists as well, that of relapse. The spouse, in attempts to avert any possibility of triggering off using behaviors, frequently avoids any perceived verbal or non-verbal behavior creating a large measure of emotional distance. The co-dependent may develop physical symptoms such as severe backaches, vague aches and pains, or psychological symptoms such as acute anxiety or depression in the initial recovery phase. His greatest fear, and sometimes greatest desire, is that the chemically dependent will begin using again.

Initially, conflict between spouses is avoided at all costs. The co-dependent fears triggering off relapse and the chemically dependent fears losing control. Since self-esteem has been conditional and directed toward efforts with the spouse, to risk conflict is to risk further emotional alienation and a decrease in acceptance. Paradoxically, the greater the efforts to avoid conflict, the more intense the conflict will be when it inevitably occurs. Such intensity reinforces the belief that conflict should be avoided at all costs because it only leads to major problems. Both the chemically dependent and co-dependent are usually secretly struggling with the overwhelming sense of loss of control, each from their own perspective. The threat of conflict tends more often to intensify the possible loss of control even further. The control paradigm is frequently magnified by competitiveness between spouses for the "one-up" position. This is a covert issue and a hidden agenda which when postulated openly is usually, vehemently denied by both spouses. This conflict is typically managed in a non-verbal, passive-aggressive manner which exacerbates emotional distance.

Another significant issue that recovering couples face is rigid pride structures (Bepko and Kreston, 1985). As emotional vulnerability increases and self-worth diminishes, the likelihood of retreat into rigid role structures and expectations increases. Each person in their own way becomes entrenched in pride responses then create further empasses for conflict resolution. Each spouse has tremendous need to view themselves as good even at the expense of their partner's self-esteem. With anger, resentment, rage, and guilt threatening the perception of good, attempts to control these feelings only serve to threaten an already fragile self-concept. Working with pride structures is often a lengthy and complex process.

Identification and expression of feelings by the recovering couple is another critical area of concern. Because self-disclosure tends to heighten emotional vulnerability, it is considered a liability rather than a valuable asset. Clinically speaking, the process of paradox is a prominent factor in the emotional life of a recovering couple. The harder one attempts to control or suppress the feelings, the more prominent they become in the context of self. Both spouses typically must face five basic feeling states experientially in recovery: anger, guilt, vulnerability, fear, and inadequacy. Each feeling, unless addressed, strongly contributes to extreme forms of coping behavior.

Leisure and recreation skills seem to be the most discounted of the four critical recovery areas by both couples and clinicians. Since this writer could find nothing in the literature to support this observation, the importance of this recovery area stands only on the merits of this writer's observation. Given the intensity of the previously mentioned issues (poor self-concept, conflict and emotional issues), stress levels run inordinately high and outlets for stress reduction are virtually non-existent or re-directed into previous unhealthy patterns such as hard work, withdrawal, or socialization structured to avoid interaction between spouses. Thus, coping patterns become the cycles by which stress is increased rather than diminished.

COUPLES' GROUP THERAPY

The challenge posed in working with recovering couples in a group setting may be accurately described by the paraphrase of a nationally known head coach: "My job is to get a group of couples to do what they don't want to do so they can achieve what they have wanted all their lives." While the treatment of the chemically dependent is becoming more refined and consistent in the first ninety days of sobriety, treatment beyond that period and particularly couples' treatment remains a relatively untapped area of clinical intervention or emphasis. The recovering couple is particularly challenging to the clinician because any expressed motivation to change is hampered by an almost total paucity of knowledge and experience of healthy functioning. The group milieu therefore must introduce some model or structure for healthy behavior. The milieu should also include a blend of psychological safety, permission to risk new behaviors, and a vital, productive tension which challenges each person and each couple without becoming threatening.

Goals of Couples' Group Therapy

To prioritize and focus dyadic energy: The marital system, as previously mentioned, is in a state of chaotic transition during initial recovery. It is necessary to provide couples with a sense of direction and common purpose. Emphasis on self-concept, conflict resolution, feeling issues, and stress reduction provides a broad but well defined area of focus for the couple.

To shift the marital system to a pro-active status rather than a reactive status: During pre-sobriety, each spouse developed defensive patterns in response to perceived psychological threats. This behavior carries over into the sobriety period and spouses often remain stuck in their defensive patterns. Spouses trained to take initiative in their own behalf often begin initiating different interactional patterns in the relationship which can lead to healthier functioning.

To understand dysfunction in the context of patterns rather than random, unpredictable events: Because of the reactive nature of the chemically dependent marriage, spouses often feel at the mercy of their spouse's behavior. As patterns are explained and identified, spouses can determine their role in formation and perpetuation of their spouse's responses. Thus, an avenue is created for each spouse to assume responsibility for their own behavior without a major threat to their respective pride structures.

To identify and distinguish realistic and unrealistic expectations of self and spouse: The recovering couple lacking a model for healthy functioning, often distort expectations of themselves and their spouse. Clarification of personal capabilities, limitations, strengths and meaningful conjoint priorities need to be acknowledged and brought to awareness for each couple in the context of their unique adjustment patterns.

To desensitize self and spouse to appropriate self-disclosure: Self-disclosure is frequently perceived as detrimental and a liability by each spouse. Both will need to experience the process in a manner that will diffuse fear and defensiveness. The process of self-disclosure is most effectively taught using indirect methods since so many defenses are marshalled around it.

To develop an awareness of the Post-Acute or Protracted Withdrawal Syndrome: Several authors (Milam and Ketcham, 1981; Gorski and Miller, 1982) have emphasized the potential contribution of the PAW Syndrome in the relapse patterns of the chemically dependent and the co-dependent. The intermittent recurrence of mood disorders, fragmented thinking, and memory loss during recovery can be misinterpreted by the chemically dependent as indicators of severe psychiatric disturbance, e.g., "I thought I was crazy for sure," is a common statement by the chemically dependent. The co-dependent may accuse her spouse of using again since the symptoms closely mimic using behavior such as blackouts, emotional withdrawal and denial. Education to this process is certainly critical knowledge for the couple and is frequently neglected by clinicians in their treatment of recovering couples.

To identify and negotiate power and control issues in the marriage: This issue is often a strong hidden agenda in recovery. The newly, sober spouse either is ready to prove his ability to fulfill his role expectations or will attempt to avoid them. In a complimentary fashion, the co-dependent spouse will either expect his spouse to assume her duties or attempt to block her efforts. In either case, the objective is to assist the couple in finding ways to negotiate and rebalance this conflictive issue.

To directly address the issue of relapse: This is undoubtedly the greatest fear of the co-dependent since he tends to pin most of the expectations for change on his spouse. Once he learns that he has control over reverting into previously dysfunctional patterns and has developed alternative responses, this fear is often greatly diminished. The greatest amount of effective work on relapse is done with the co-dependent rather than the chemically dependent.

To identify and develop "markers" for progress and success unique to each couple: Since the couple has been lacking in a model for healthy functioning, couples' work can seem overwhelming and never-ending. Couples need to have some idea on a relatively frequent basis when they are making progress. The therapist can shift strokes for progress in particular areas to markers of success, e.g., "Your (the couple) use of 'I' statements is increasing. This is a strong indicator of progress for the both of you. What types of differences do you experience in your marriage when you use 'I' messages?''

To develop reciprocal, healthy validation between spouses: Psychological defenses and pride structures of the couple are initially deeply entrenched and rigid. To offer and accept compliments and positive strokes often shifts the sense of self-identity from a "doing" perspective to that of "being." The couple is taught statements such as, "I appreciate your ability to deal with our finances," and confronted on the discounting defenses which typically follow.

Group Structure

Introducing the group: This writer immediately re-frames the group as a "sharing or discussion" group rather than a "couples' therapy group." This subtle shift in perspective accommodates a more relaxed, less clinical atmosphere and sets the tone for a psychologically protected environment. It detracts from the notion of pathology, being clinically labelled and forced to "spill my guts in front of strangers" as one patient explained his initial refusal to participate.

Group Size

Five to six couples provide a maximum opportunity for effective group interaction. Any more than this diffuses the sense of psychological safety.

Therapist Qualifications

This type of group requires a therapist skilled in marital therapy, oriented to systemic therapies, and experienced in the group setting. A male/female co-facilitator structure is ideal to provide effective modeling and to cue into gender-specific issues. The skill of the therapist is most critical in developing a delicate balance where marital therapy and self-disclosure require therapeutic balance in the group setting. Too deep into therapy and group members become easily threatened; too shallow and they may not gain from the session. For example, discussing sexual issues in the group will weaken the prospect for self-disclosure. Couples should be directed to marital therapy for such issues. Discussion of the divorce rate in America is equally inappropriate, lacking relevance to the specific needs of the group. Since this balance utilizes intuitive therapeutic processes, the therapist must often draw on an extensive history of marital therapy skills.

Selection of Participants

The therapist will need to consider the couples' group as a speciality group, subordinate in priority to the primary commitments of AA and Al-Anon. Several criteria should be considered in selecting couples for the group.

1. A strong commitment to AA and Al-Anon activities as evidenced by weekly participation of each spouse.
2. The couple are living together and are not separated or filing for divorce.
3. A willingness to commit to weekly participation for a twelve-week period.
4. Have at least one month of regular participation in AA or Al-Anon groups.

The therapist selecting couples may want to evaluate poor prognosis vs. favorable prognosis couples. Those couples with a poor prognosis for couples' group should be referred for marital therapy. The literature reflects a fair amount of research on chemical dependency and outcome of marital status. Couples who rate highest on hostile and coercive interactions prior to treatment have been found to have the poorest treatment outcomes (Moos, Bromet, Tsu and Moos, 1979; Orford, Oppenheimer, Egert and Hensman, 1977). Evidence suggests that wives were more likely to request and be granted separation from their alcoholic husbands the more they have been exposed to hardship or deviance within the marriage (Haberman, 1965; Jackson and Kogan, 1963). The clinical implications of some research findings (Orford et al., 1976) suggest that treatment centered on symptoms alone of the patient or spouse is insufficient in instances where a breakdown in marital cohesion exists. Family participation by the husband, favorability of the wife's perception of the husband, and frequency of nurtural demonstrations of affection are strongly indicated as cohesive elements in the marriage (Orford et al., 1976). This writer has found several symptomatic processes that indicate a poor prognosis for recovering couples in the first year of sobriety:

1. Lack of commitment by at least one spouse to attend recovery activities.
2. Emotional apathy or ambivalence toward the behavior of a spouse that remains unchangeable.
3. Consistent discounting or denial by a spouse of his partner's internal experiences.
4. A history of severe emotional and/or physical abuse.
5. A history of severe manipulations, i.e., threats of suicide, homicide, etc.
6. Independent lifestyles of spouses that promote a lack of common interests or purpose.
7. One spouse actively involved in an affair.
8. One or more spouses have a hidden agenda for getting out of the marriage.
9. One or more spouses manifest strong denial of emotional dependency on the other.

Some clinicians have argued that couples should not be treated until at least six months into sobriety. This gives the couple time, it is believed, for problems to resolve themselves as part of the natural recovery process. This writer has found that couples can be treated as early as a month into sobriety as long as they demonstrate consistency of commitment to their respective recovery programs as evidenced by their regular attendance at AA and Al-Anon meetings. Motivated couples demonstrate an eagerness to learn healthier and more effective ways of relating to each other. Due to their history of dysfunction, couples do not have the luxury of relying on "natural" processes to resolve marital impasses. The concept of "natural and normal" require some definition and structure in order to be used successfully by the recovering couple. A time factor for implementing couples' work is of lesser priority than other critical factors such as level of commitment to the marriage, marital cohesiveness and motivation for change by one or both of the spouses.

INTERVENTION TECHNIQUES

Theme-Centered Problem Solving

The four areas of recovery previously reviewed represent specific themes in the initial year of sobriety on which the couple can focus their efforts. Paolino and McCrady (1977) have suggested that theme-centered problem solving represents an effective method of integrating behavior approaches with psychoanalytic and/or systems approaches which emphasize the unconscious determinants of marital conflicts. Theme-centered problem solving also diffuses these emotionally volatile issues in such a way that couples can relate to how a particular theme may relate to their unique circumstances. Theme examples could include fear of loss of control, unrealistic expectations, chronic blaming, anger and resentments, etc. Group sessions can then be guided to generate solutions and alternative approaches related to the particular theme of the session.

Structuring

Perhaps the most frequent, ineffective assumption many clinicians make about recovering couples' groups is that group interaction can evolve from a spontaneous "here and now" format. Although couples may demonstrate strong motivation and profess the desire to work on the marriage, this intent is often powerfully conflicted. The fear of self-disclosure, the repressed negative feelings, and heightened psychological defenses frequently leave couples silent and resistant to discussion. Sessions can be structured by using theme oriented open-ended questions. Sentence completion and brief survey materials can be helpful in generating group discussion. Examples might include:

"Several ways misunderstandings occur in a marriage are. . . ."

"The two biggest problems for a recovering couple in the first three months of sobriety are. . . ."

"What is the difference between anger, hate, and resentment?"

Prescribing the Pattern

This paradoxical technique challenges couples to "make up a pattern" by which they could create the most effective argument. Included would be emotional payoffs, myths of change, and hidden agendas. This technique tends to work best after couples are well bonded emotionally into the group. It should be attempted by a therapist quite familiar with the use of paradoxical technique. Alternative responses to the patterns can be brainstormed by group members who assist the working couple to "find a way to break the pattern."

Developing a "Care Manual" for Your Spouse

Couples are given several major areas of marital adjustment related to recovery, e.g., trust, self-esteem, mutual respect, etc. Each spouse is then directed to answer the question, "I feel my spouse loves me when he says . . . , or does . . ." as it relates to each major area. Responses must be specific, observable, and measurable. Once the lists are completed, spouses then exchange their "Caring Manuals" with the acknowledgement that each spouse is identifying the necessary behaviors to help them feel cared for and loved by their spouse.

Regardless of technique, the clinician needs to keep several critical factors foremost in their thinking with regard to therapeutic efforts. These points have been previously emphasized in the literature (Paolino and McCrady, 1977). Because the chemically dependent marital system is fragile and extremely limited with regard to adaptive means of coping with threats to homeostasis, therapy needs to be gradually and slowly applied, and not directed at efforts to change large segments of dysfunctional behavior in brief spans of time. Secondly, chemically dependent couples should be approached with recognition and appreciation for the emotional components of behavior. Finally, regardless of the theoretical perspective of the clinician, she should, when therapeutically appropriate, attempt to establish the meaningfulness of unconscious thoughts, feelings, and mental processes through the techniques of interpretation or cognitive reframing.

CONCLUSION

This article has explained therapy with recovering couples in a group milieu. The foundation for this work lies in systems theory and emphasized four basic areas on which the clinician should focus with the recovering couple in the first year of sobriety: self-concept, conflict management, identification and expression of feelings, and leisure and recreational skills. The goals of couples' group therapy were identified and couples with poor prognosis were discussed. Techniques of intervention were presented with emphasis on more structured rather than spontaneous processes.

Clinical efforts in working with recovering couples are still in the early phases of development. Much remains to be done in the refinement of therapeutic approaches. Far from any definitive notions, this article represents a point of departure from which, hopefully, others will follow in the challenge of working with this complex but rewarding population in the field of chemical dependency.

BIBLIOGRAPHY

R. Beavers, *Successful Marriage: A Family Systems Approach to Couples Therapy*, W. W. Norton & Co., New York, 1985.

C. Bepko & J. Krestan, *The Responsibility Trap: A Blueprint for Treating the Alcoholic Family*, The Free Press, New York, 1985.

D. Berenson, *Alcohol and the Family System*, M. P. Guerin (Ed.), "Family Therapy: Theory and Practice," pp. 284-297, Gardner Press, New York, 1976.

L. Bertalanfly, *General Systems Theory*, George Braziller, New York, 1968.

M. Bowen, *Changing Families: A Family Therapy Reader*, "The Use of Family Theory in Clinical Practice," M. J. Haley (Ed.), Grune & Stratton, New York, 1971.

G. Burton & H. M. Kaplan, "Marriage Counseling With Alcoholics and Their Spouses. The Correlation of Excessive Drinking Behavior With Family Pathology and Social Deterioration," *British Journal of Addictions*, *63*, pp. 161-170, 1968.

P. M. Gallant, A. Rich, E. Bey, & L. Terranova, "Group Psychotherapy With Married Couples: A Successful Technique in New Orleans Alcoholism Clinic Patients," *Journal of Louisiana Medical Society*, *122*, pp. 41-44, 1970.

S. K. Geiss & D. K. O'Leary, "Therapist Ratings of Frequency and Severity of Marital Problems: Implications for Research," *Journal of Marital and Family Therapy*, *7*, pp. 515-520, 1981.

T. Gorski & M. Miller, *Counseling for Relapse Prevention*, Independence Press, Independence, Missouri, 1982.

P. W. Haberman, "Some Characteristics of Alcoholic Marriages Differentiated by Level of Deviance," *Journal of Marriage and the Family*, 27, pp. 34-36, 1965.

J. K. Jackson & K. L. Kogan, "The Search for Solutions in Help Seeing Patterns of Families of Active and Inactive Alcoholics," *Quarterly Journal of Studies on Alcohol*, 24, pp. 440-472, 1963.

B. S. McCrady, "Marital Dysfunction: Alcoholism and Marriage," E. Kaufman & E. M. Pattison (Eds.), *Encyclopedia Handbook of Alcoholism*, pp. 673-685, Gardner Press, New York, 1982.

J. Milam & K. Ketcham, *Under the Influence*, Bantam Books, New York, 1981.

R. H. Moos, E. Bromet, V. Tsu, & B. Moos, "Family Characteristics and the Outcome of Treatment for Alcoholism," *Journal of Studies on Alcohol*, 40, pp. 78-88, 1979.

J. Orford, E. Oppenheimer, S. Egert, C. Hensman, & S. Guthrie, "The Cohesiveness of Alcoholism-Complicated Marriages and Its Influence on Treatment Outcome," *British Journal of Psychiatry*, 128, pp. 318-339, 1976.

J. Orford, E. Oppenheimer, S. Egert, & C. Hensman, "The Role of Excessive Drinking in Alcoholism-Complicated Marriages: A Study of Stability and Change Over a One-year Period," *International Journal of Addiction*, 12, pp. 471-495, 1977.

T. Paolino & B. S. McCrady, "Joint Admission as a Treatment Modality for Problem Drinkers: A Case Report," *American Journal of Psychiatry*, 133, pp. 222-224, 1976.

T. Paolino & B. S. McCrady, *The Alcoholic Marriage: Alternative Perspectives*, Grune & Stratton, New York, 1977.

C. G. Smith, "Alcoholics: Their Treatment and Their Wives," *British Journal of Psychiatry*, 115, pp. 1039-1042, 1969.

P. Steinglass, S. Weiner, & J. Mendelson, "A Systems Approach to Alcoholism. A Model and Its Clinical Application," *Archives of General Psychiatry*, 24, pp. 401-408, 1971.

S. Wegscheider, *Another Chance*, Science and Behavior Books, Palo Alto, California, 1981.

Outpatient Co-dependency Treatment

Ronald T. Potter-Efron, PhD, CAC
Patricia S. Potter-Efron, BA, CAC

INTRODUCTION

A twelve week outpatient treatment program for co-dependency that combines education, individual therapy and group therapy is described below. This program accepts affected adult children, spouses/partners/former partners, and parents of alcoholics or chemically dependent individuals. It is based on the premises that co-dependent persons have both the right and the capacity to make fundamental changes in their self-concept, world view and daily behaviors and that these changes can occur without regard to whether or how the alcoholic changes. The program neither requires nor anticipates participation from the alcoholic or other family members, although children of the co-dependents are invited to one educational session and the alcoholic may be seen separately or in couples sessions during the twelve weeks. Participants are informed that even small changes on their part are likely to produce strong family resistance and other less predictable family responses; they are encouraged to view these reactions as indicators of their own movement rather than as messages that they must stop growing.

This co-dependency treatment program is designed to effect change in four major spheres: behavior, cognition, affect, and spirituality. Specific goals in these areas are described later in this paper. The program also addresses the eight content areas described in the co-dependency assessment article that appears elsewhere in this

---

Ronald T. Potter-Efron is affiliated with the Midelfort Clinic, and Patricia S. Potter-Efron is in private practice, both in Eau Claire, WI.

151

volume: fear, shame/guilt, prolonged despair, anger, denial, rigidity, impaired identity development and confusion. Specific educational and clinical information with regard to these areas is also provided here.

Participants in the co-dependency program attend one two-hour assessment/screening interview, six one-hour individual therapy sessions, eight one-hour educational lectures, and sixteen two-hour group therapy sessions (two sessions per week for the first month along with the educational sessions). Thus, the first four weeks represent an intensive phase of the program while the remaining eight weeks provide an opportunity for the participants to put into practice their changes and to return weekly to the group for support and validation.

SCREENING CONCERNS

Before admission each potential participant completes a two-hour screening interview. The co-dependency assessment questionnaire printed earlier in this volume is administered during this interview. Relevant current and historical information is gathered with regard to the client's experience living with alcoholics or in other highly stressful family situations. Particular attention is also paid to the client's medical history (stress related illnesses), alcohol/drug use, and psychiatric counseling history.

Clients who are accepted into the program range from individuals just introduced to the concept of co-dependency to those who have extensive experience with the concept through Al-Anon or previous counseling. Clients also vary on their degree of current crisis: adult children with deceased parents or ex-partners not currently involved in a dysfunctional living situation tend to be the least crisis oriented while others are in the midst of immediate, overwhelming troubles. Nevertheless, a common denominator for almost all clients is a sense of being trapped—physically, emotionally, or cognitively, unable to extricate themselves from deeply engrained patterns of activity and relationship.

Candidates are screened out of the program for several reasons: (1) they may be assessed as not having enough of the characteristics of co-dependency to merit inclusion; (2) they may be co-dependent but have another problem that must be given priority: chemical dependency, organic depression, etc.; (3) they may need intensive individual therapy before they could benefit from a group format; (4) they may have done enough work previously on their co-dependency that they would benefit more from participation in other therapy opportunities.

PROGRAM GOALS

Recovery from co-dependency is conceptualized as a wholistic process that involves a general reorganization of the client's world view. Specific concepts and guidelines are provided to help clients restructure their lives but more emphasis is placed upon this overall personal revision than on a presentation of the "do's and don'ts" of co-dependent life. Clients are informed of our expectation that most of them will begin to find their own way out of the traps they are in by the end of the program. We are careful to indicate that getting out of the trap does not necessarily mean leaving the alcoholic. Thus, responsibility for recovery is left with the client since no specific demands for that recovery are dictated by the therapists.

Clients are shown the general and specific goals listed in Table I. Comments about these goals are made below.

OVERALL GOAL

We believe that the general goal for co-dependent clients is essentially identical to that for most clients in chemical health or mental health settings. Our hope is that these persons will leave the program with greater self-respect, more self-awareness, an improved ability to care for themselves, and with the capacity to enter into positive relationships with others in which their own identities are neither submerged nor distorted. To facilitate these changes more concrete and specific tasks are designated under the headings of behavioral, cognitive, affective and spiritual goals.

TABLE I

Goals: Co-Dependency Program

Date _____
Name _____   Week in Treatment _____
D.O.B. _____   Discharge Date _____
Staff Members Present: _____

OVERALL GOAL: The individual who completes this program will become a detached and caring person who respects and understands herself or himself, and who is capable of developing in-depth relationships based upon the principle of mutual interdependence.

SPECIFIC GOALS	COMMENTS/OBSERVATIONS/ REVISIONS

Behavioral

1. To attend program regularly.
2. To attend Al-Anon at least one time per week.
3. To complete assignments on time.
4. To practice appropriate self-care in daily behavior.
5. To practice principles of detachment in daily behavior.
6. To practice principles of mutual interdependence in significant relationships.
7.

Cognitive

1. To understand and accept the disease concept of alcoholism.
2. To gain awareness of the effects alcohol/drugs have had upon the co-dependent individual.
3. To understand and accept the concepts of detachment, individuation and boundary settings.
4. To understand and accept the concepts of mutuality and interdependence in relationship.

TABLE I (continued)

SPECIFIC GOALS	COMMENTS/OBSERVATIONS/ REVISIONS
5. To develop an increased capacity to gather and sort data, coming to consistent decisions based on realistic criteria (vs. confusion, indecisiveness and gullibility). 6.	

Affective

1. To identify own feelings and be aware of them as they occur.
2. To practice sharing feelings with peers, family, and staff.
3. To understand how one's feelings have been/are affected by co-dependent relationships.
4. To develop the capacity to be responsible only for one's own feelings and to detach from the feelings of others.
5.

Spiritual

1. To replace hopelessness and despair with an appropriate sense of hope.
2. To replace feelings of shame and deficiency with a sense of self-worth and belonging in the world.
3. To review and modify one's value system to support personal self-respect and mutual relationships.
4. To review and develop a personal relationship with the Higher Power as understood by the individual.
5.

DISCUSSION/DISCHARGE PLANS:

COGNITIVE GOALS

In order for individuals to change in a consistent manner it is usually helpful for them to have an organized model that provides direction. The model utilized in this program focuses upon the individuation/differentiation process (Bowen; Kerr), a family therapy approach that places emphasis upon the individual's need to gain emotional neutrality about his or her family of origin by recognizing its multiple systemic interactions. One goal of this therapy model is to help individuals differentiate themselves from others so that they can maintain emotional autonomy in a relationship system (Kerr, p. 9). Differentiation of self actually improves the person's capacity for significant interaction since it allows the individual to make meaningful choices about how and with whom to interact. In this model a healthy functioning person is one who has a realistic understanding of self both historically and in the present, an ability to stand alone in the world but also the capacity to experience intimacy with others. As Kerr states, "Systems theory encompasses both individuality and togetherness" (Kerr, p. 22).

Individuation is a process quite difficult for co-dependent clients, many of whom grew up in deeply enmeshed or emotionally distant families. At a cognitive level participants must be given information that differentiation is possible as well as desirable. Furthermore, this process usually must be begun in the client's current family or relationship situation, especially with those living with practicing alcoholics.

Fortunately, the Al-Anon principle of "detachment" provides the vehicle to introduce the concepts of individuation and differentiation. Although there is no single definition of this concept (the Al-Anon "Bible," *One Day At A Time in Al-Anon*, lists twenty-one separate entries on the topic, all of which are distinct) the concept includes the essential features of differentiation: the right to care for self, the need to gain emotional distance from the alcoholic, responsibility for self instead of others. As long as differentiation is distinguished from emotional or physical abandonment of the alcoholic this concept can be used as a bridge between the professional and self-help communities and as a central cognitive principle for program participants.

Another aspect of differentiation theory, the concept of triangulation, has been modified for use in co-dependency treatment. Triangulation refers to a tendency for relationships between two persons to become three sided with the introduction of a second parent, sibling or child. For example, a conversation between a couple about the wife's drinking may be interrupted by a child whose primary concern is to keep the peace and preserve the marriage. Relatively healthy families are those in which each member can have non-triangulated interactions with all others.

We use this process metaphorically to illustrate the "Detachment Triangle," a model that helps participants recognize their overinvolvement with the alcoholic. As can be seen in Illustration I, the co-dependent before treatment tends to be overly involved with the alcoholic in the alcoholic role but to have forgotten how to relate to that individual as a human being. For example, an adult child of an alcoholic may refuse to be around her sober father because of painful memories or because of the fear that he will drink later. Co-dependents also tend to become so involved in attempting to modify or control the alcoholic's drinking that they assume there is no internal dialogue going on within the mind of that alcoholic with regard to his drinking behavior.

Illustration II represents a different and healthier version of this triangle that we present to the participants. In this figure the co-dependent individual has returned attention to the significant other as a human being. In order to do so the participants must complete a three step process: (1) "detach" from the alcoholic by having less interaction with the actively using significant other (in other words, "don't argue with a drunk"); (2) find ways to relate to the significant other as a human being (such as seeing that person mostly when sober or remembering positive interactions) and/or mourn the loss of that human being; (3) allow the alcoholic to have his own internal conflict about drinking without attempting to interfere. We have found this new triangle to be attractive to co-dependents because it offers a trade off; instead of thinking of detachment simply as a withdrawal process (saying goodbye to the alcoholic) the individual may also move toward the more positive aspects of that person. When used in a group in which designated members play out the roles of alcoholic and human being with the co-dependent, this particular cognitive reframing can also have a powerful emotional impact on clients.

ILLUSTRATION I

Detachment Triangle: Overinvolvement Phase

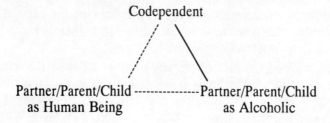

Codependent

Partner/Parent/Child ---------------- Partner/Parent/Child
as Human Being   as Alcoholic

ILLUSTRATION II

Detachment Triangle: Detached Phase

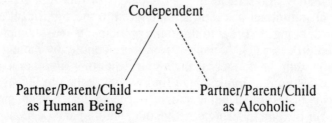

Codependent

Partner/Parent/Child ---------------- Partner/Parent/Child
as Human Being   as Alcoholic

Key:

-------------- = Tenuous Connection
_____ = Normal Connection
_____ = Overly Connected

The list of cognitive goals begins with helping group members achieve an understanding of how alcohol has affected both the alcoholic and the family. We utilize the disease concept and standard family therapy concepts to portray the typical situation in which all players in the family dramas become focused upon the alcoholic. The third and fourth listed goals encourage participants in both aspects of the differentiation process, namely learning to exist alone and in relationships.

The fifth goal, "to develop an increased capacity to gather and sort data, coming to consistent decisions based on realistic criteria" is a recognition that many co-dependents struggle with an inability to think clearly. Confusion, uncertainty and indecisiveness frequently accompany growing up or living in a family that survives on denial of reality, responsibility shifts, double messages, and other "crazy-making" activities. One method that we have used to help participants gain greater confidence in their ability to think involves group validation of a client's perceptions, which is perhaps the most important value of the group process. Another technique is the presentation of Albert Ellis' irrational beliefs (Ellis) which helps clients identify their exaggerated and inaccurate assumptions about the world. The crucial message for co-dependents is that they do have the ability to think clearly and to act upon those thoughts.

BEHAVIORAL TASKS AND GOALS

We view detachment partially as a pragmatic set of behaviors that promote individuation and differentiation. Every act of self-care is encouraged, beginning with regular attendance at the group and individual sessions and at Al-Anon. Since family members often strongly resist the participant's therapy, attendance itself is defined as evidence that the individual has indeed begin self-nurturance.

Self-care is distinguished both from "self-less" and "self-ish" behavior. "Self-lessness" occurs whenever individuals ignore or deny their own wants and needs. These persons may have been taught in their families of origin that any act of self-care is "self-ish"; therefore their goal is to eliminate their own unacceptable desires. Co-dependent clients tend to feel guilty whenever they want something for themselves. To minimize this guilt they focus upon the needs of others. They may store resentment that nobody appreciates them but fail to recognize that others will not respect persons who do not respect themselves. Positive self-care is demonstrated by such activities as taking fifteen minutes each day for oneself (Drews), enrolling in education or activity programs, relaxation or meditation training, recreational pursuits, etc. Energy formerly consumed in co-dependent overconcern for the user is in this manner rechanneled into productive self-nurturing daily activity.

Assignments consist of readings on detachment and the completion of the Family First Step as well as individually designed homework tasks. The Family First Step again helps the participants detach from the user, this time by concentrating attention upon the uselessness of trying to run somebody else's life. The primary message is that "we are powerless over someone else's use of alcohol and that our lives have become unmanageable." This step is discussed in greater detail elsewhere (Potter-Efron & Potter-Efron, 1986).

Behaviorally, detachment is noted by a reduction in actions that protect a user from the consequences of his drinking or irresponsibility. Examples include refusing to give money to an adolescent to buy drugs and not making excuses for the alcoholic to other family members. Combined with positive self-care, these behaviors help participants fundamentally reshape their daily routines during the co-dependency treatment program.

The final behavioral goal is for participants to practice principles of mutual interdependence in significant relationships. Interdependence is defined as action occurring between two persons in which both individuals have significant input, negotiations occur from a base of mutual respect and, most importantly, both persons are capable of existing independently but choose to rely upon each other to improve the quality of their lives. The state of interdependence is contrasted with dependence, counterdependence, and independence. Dependence occurs when individuals rely upon others for their basic self-worth or identity; co-dependents tend to become emotionally dependent upon others in this manner since they often have an external locus of control (Smalley). While the alcoholic depends upon the co-dependent for physical support, the co-dependent depends upon the alcoholic to supply purpose in living and approval. Counter-dependent behavior happens when co-dependents rebel against their dependency. While dependent individuals have difficulty saying "no" to their partners, counter-dependent individuals refuse to say "yes." They are still trapped with the alcoholic since they must continually monitor him to know when to be angry with him. Independent behavior develops when these persons become capable of making decisions based upon their own needs and perceptions and when they become capable of living alone.

We have found that many of the participants in the co-dependency program have become stuck in dependent or counter-dependent relationships with their partners, parents or children. Our initial concern is to encourage independent behavior. Once independence is established attention can then be directed toward encouraging interdependent relationships. Since most active alcoholics are incapable of interdependence participants are urged to practice this new kind of relationship with each other and with friends and family.

AFFECTIVE GOALS

Co-dependent individuals, because they live in chronic highly stressful situations, often have difficulty recognizing or expressing a full range of feelings. Recognizing feelings may produce a strong desire to live differently, but since co-dependents often believe they are caught in an unalterable family trap, it becomes more efficient to deny or minimize feelings. Also, free expression of affect is only possible in a safe environment. When co-dependents attempt to express their feelings within an alcoholic family they may be met with ridicule, disinterest, or violence. Eventually these persons learn to "stuff" their feelings in order to keep the peace.

The affective goals in our program reflect a need to provide a safe environment in which participants can explore their feelings. Many secrets get shared, sometimes for the first time. These new revelations ease the isolation of co-dependents who may think that only they have rageful thoughts or have acted irrationally or immorally in the past. Participants are urged to keep a regular diary of their feelings during the twelve weeks so that they become more skilled at recognizing their feelings.

Individuation/differentiation is sought at the affect level as well as in behavior and cognition. It is particularly difficult for co-dependents to accept responsibility only for their own feelings. Shifting responsibility for feelings is routine in alcoholic families. For example, the alcoholic might argue that "you made me angry enough to drink," giving away responsibility both for his feelings and his behavior. In turn, co-dependents may claim that the alcoholic makes them sad, mad, scared, etc. Again, responsibility is shifted. Emotions then become treated as "passions," something passively suffered by the victim of somebody else's behavior (Averill, p. 13). Co-dependents and alcoholics can both then perceive themselves as innocent victims, helpless to effect their feelings. As long as this attitude is maintained these individuals will be unable to differentiate. Therapeutically it is not enough for participants just to share feelings. They must additionally be helped to take ownership of those feelings and to return to the alcoholic responsibility for his emotions.

Five specific affects are handled in lectures and group assignments: fear, shame, guilt, despair, and anger. For an explanation of the significance of these emotions in co-dependency the reader is referred to the article on co-dependency assessment that appears in this volume. What follows are treatment concerns that are approached during therapy.

Co-dependent individuals face a host of complicated fears: death or injury of the alcoholic, abandonment, loss of control of the situation, loss of trust for the alcoholic or others, physical violence. Many of these fears are realistic and must be treated with respect. For this reason we do not try to talk participants out of their fears. Instead, we suggest that courage is defined as taking appropriate action even though one is afraid. Especially when there is a legitimate risk of violence we encourage clients to "pick your fights carefully" so that they can maximize positive changes in their lives. Individuals with a history of panic attacks or chronic anxiety may also be referred for psychiatric evaluation. In general participants do become less fearful over time as they experience group acceptance and success in self-nurturing behaviors.

Exposure of shameful episodes in a supportive environment is a necessary component for shame work. Co-dependent clients tend to reveal these secrets slowly. For this reason the treatment program is "layered" with opportunities for progressively deeper revelations during the twelve weeks. Initial efforts are basically invitations for the participants just to talk about themselves. Later, specific exercises such as one in which individuals first draw their "masks" and then their real selves allow greater risk taking. Individual therapy sessions also present an opportunity for participants to test the acceptability of their shameful secrets with the therapist before they share with the group. Highly confrontative attacks on clients are never used since these tactics only tend to produce more shame.

Co-dependent individuals are frequently guilt laden. This is partly a boundary issue in that co-dependents tend to assume guilt for the behavior and pain of others. This type of guilt is irrational (Forrest, Ellis) and one important task in treatment is to help participants separate any rational guilt they have about their behavior from these irrational feelings and thoughts.

Even when these persons have actually done something that merits a guilty response they may greatly exaggerate its significance. Co-dependents may believe that anything they do wrong is horrible and demonstrates their basic inadequacy to the world. Here the therapeutic task is to help the individual recognize that everybody errs — to accept themselves as fallible but essentially good human beings. Co-dependents must be able to forgive themselves in order to accept themselves.

Finally, anticipatory guilt serves as a brake against co-dependents taking positive action. Contemplating taking even a few minutes for themselves participants in the group often feel guilt, apparently because self-care violates family norms. The basic message to these clients in this situation is that they can only grow if they act on their own behalf despite this guilt. Group encouragement and stories of successful accomplishment of self-nurturing tasks helps clients act through their guilt instead of being deterred by it. The group can also help with guilt experienced by participants after they do positive things for themselves.

Despair seems to be an emotion that combines a sense of desperation with a mood of helplessness. This situation is common in alcoholic families. Members of these families may feel trapped, watching helplessly as their lives become less manageable. No longer able even to sustain the illusion that can control the alcoholic, co-dependents may gradually give up.

Individuation is a key to renewing hope. When participants are able to focus upon themselves they may then discover how to improve the quality of their lives in ways that do not depend upon the recovery or cooperation of the alcoholic. With despair the therapeutic sequence starts with helping clients recognize and share their pain, then accepting that despair as a legitimate reaction to what appears to be a hopeless situation, and then pointing clients toward a new and meaningful direction as a way out of the trap that they may not have noticed before. This third step works best when it is offered only as an invitation by the therapists; any attempts to force the participants to attend to themselves may be interpreted as attacks on the alcoholic and then rejected. However, because co-dependents who seek treatment have already signalled their need for guidance we have found most eager to shed their despair and move toward hope.

Anger is the last feeling specifically targeted in this treatment program. Co-dependent anger occurs regularly. Like most anger, it is a signal that something is wrong that alerts, motivates, and invigorates individuals to defend their basic interests (Gaylin, p. 52). Although difficult to manage, anger can be a tool for change ". . . when it challenges us to become more of an expert on the self and less of an expert on others" (Lerner, p. 102).

A disproportionate number of co-dependents appear to be angerphobic, that is habitually afraid to express feelings of anger because of fear of loss of control or abandonment. Others have become addicted to anger, becoming angry or even rageful without sufficient provocation. Anger phobic and addicted co-dependents are introduced to assertiveness training during the program. The goal is to help them express their anger in an appropriate manner. Ventilation techniques, such as having a client hit a punching bag, are used occasionally with anger phobic persons so that they can recognize the depths of their anger. Ventilation is not used with anger addicted individuals since that may serve only to solidify an already problematic pattern (Tavris, p. 144) of habitual anger. These individuals are helped to develop alternatives to angry outbursts such as relaxation, taking time outs, and fair fighting techniques.

SPIRITUAL GOALS

Spirituality is a broad term that is concerned with one's ability to relate to others, to self, and to a higher power as understood by that individual (Dollard, p. 7). Spirituality includes self-caring behavior, such as taking time off to relax or exercise (Whitfield, p. 53). Perhaps more importantly, it involves having a sense of meaning or purpose in life (Whitfield) and a feeling of belonging to something greater than oneself. Paradoxically, individuals who have not been able to differentiate themselves from others might have difficulty with this sense of spirituality. Feeling inadequate and incomplete they may not be aware of any internal meaning to their lives. Co-dependent persons tend to have an external locus of control (Smalley), deriving their identity from the expectations of others. A sense of belonging may accompany this identity but it is a belonging based more upon the fear of abandonment than upon free choice.

Individuals need to review their entire value system as part of their treatment for co-dependency. Values that support feelings of shame, hopelessness, despair and deficiency must be brought into the open so that the participants have the opportunity to modify them. As noted before, it is important to introduce and reinforce the value of taking care of self. Many co-dependents have developed a value system in which taking care of others has much greater importance than self-nurturance. We help clients develop an ability to care both for themselves and for others through emphasizing the value of self-care. Our goal is not to eliminate caring for others as a behavior or value but to promote an inner dialogue within the co-dependents in which both caring for self and for others are respected values. In a similar manner we attempt to create internal dialogue between optimism and pessimism so that the participants are neither one-sidedly optimistic (gullible) nor pessimistic (cynical) and between deficiency and superiority to combat both their low self-concept and the sense of superiority (grandiosity) that sometimes covers up inferiority.

Many co-dependents develop over time a spiritual bitterness and

166 CO-DEPENDENCY: ISSUES IN TREATMENT AND RECOVERY

despair. They may feel angry at God for allowing their terrible suffering, unable to comprehend why they are being punished through somebody else's alcoholism. As a result they may quit going to church or refuse to entertain spiritual questions. Co-dependents in this state may feel terribly alone, disconnected from the universe. This combination of spiritual bitterness and isolation promotes shame and guilt feelings as co-dependents drift away from their original beliefs. A vicious circle may develop because ashamed persons then run even further away to hide their shame, thus producing more bitterness and isolation.

The final goal in our co-dependency treatment program is to help participants re-examine their relationship with their higher power. In order to do so we encourage clients to attend Al-Anon regularly. We also utilize Whitfield's spirituality self-assessment scale (Whitfield), which presents a broad spectrum of spiritual questions and is non-religious in focus. Such a self-examination cannot by itself relieve the spiritual despair noted above. But it can initiate a process in which co-dependent participants will eventually feel better connected with other human beings and more content with the spiritual meaning of their lives.

CONCLUSION

We have outlined above the goals and procedures involved in a twelve week outpatient co-dependency treatment program. This program is designed primarily to promote individuation and differentiation, breaking the dependency of co-dependents upon others for self-worth. Specific goals and tasks have been included to encourage change in the four areas of cognition, behavior, affect and spirituality.

REFERENCES

Averill, James *Anger and Aggression*, New York, Springer-Verlog, 1982.
Bowen, Murray "Toward the Differentiation of Self in One's Family of Origin," in J. Framo (ed.), *Family Interaction*, New York, Springer, 1972.
Dollard, Jerry "Toward Spirituality: The Inner Journey," Center City, MN, Hazelden Press, 1983.

Drews, Toby Rice *Getting Them Sober*, vol 1 S. Plainfield, NJ: Bridge Publishing, Inc., 1980.

Ellis, Albert *How to Live With—and Without—Anger*, New York, Readers Digest Press, 1977.

Forrest, Gary *Alcoholism, Narcissism and Psychopathology*, Springfield, IL, Charles C Thomas, 1983.

Gaylin, Willard *The Rage Within*, New York, Simon and Schuster, 1984.

Kerr, Michael E. "Theoretical Base for Differentiation of Self in One's Family of Origin," New York, The Haworth Press, Inc., 1984.

Lerner, Harriet, *The Dance of Anger*, Cambridge, Harper and Row, 1985.

_____, *One Day at a Time in Al-Anon*, New York, Al-Anon Family Group Headquarters, Inc., 1985.

Potter-Efron, Patricia and Potter-Efron, Ronald "Treating the Family of the Chemically Dependent Adolescent: The Enabling Inventory and Other Techniques for Responsibility," Alcoholism Treatment Quarterly, vol 3, no. 1, Sp 1986, pp. 59-72.

Potter-Efron, Ronald and Potter-Efron, Patricia "Assessment of Codependency," Alcoholism Treatment Quarterly, pp. 37-57.

Smalley, Sondra "Co-Dependency: An Introduction," New Brighton, MN, SBS Productions, 1982.

Tavris, Carol *Anger: The Misunderstood Emotion*, New York, Simon and Schuster, 1982.

Whitfield, Charles "Stress Management and Spirituality During Recovery," Alcoholism Treatment Quarterly, vol 1, no. 1, Spring 1984, pp. 3-54.